Jolly Literacy

Reading Comprehension & Writing Skills

Teacher's Book

1

Written by
Sara Wernham

Edited by Fran Bromage

With thanks to Rachel Griffin, Becky Miles, Susan Purcell, and Susan Whittaker.

Contents

Part 1: Introduction

What is Jolly Literacy?... 3
How does Jolly Literacy link to TEFL?... 4
What is in the Reading Comprehension & Writing Skills Program?...... 4
How should the core materials be used?... 4
Texts/formats covered in Level 1... 5
Examples of unit structure in Level 1.. 6
Why is reading comprehension important?... 6
Oral development 6
A note about story time 7
How do the comprehension units work within the program?................ 7
What does the Science of Reading say about comprehension?............. 8
Why are writing skills important?.. 8
How do the writing units work within the program?............................. 8
What is the Science of Writing?... 9
Learning Objectives for Year 1 9
Help for struggling students 9
Supplementary materials 10
How to navigate a Reading Comprehension lesson
in the Student Book and in the Teacher's Book 11
How to navigate a Writing Skills lesson
in the Workbook and in the Teacher's Book... 12

Part 2: Scope & Sequence: Level 1

Weeks   1 – 12.. 13
Weeks   13 – 24 14
Weeks   25 – 36... 15

Part 3: Teaching with the Reading Comprehension Student Book and the Writing Skills Workbook

Unit 1	16	Unit 19	88
Unit 2	20	Unit 20	92
Unit 3	24	Unit 21	96
Unit 4	28	Unit 22	100
Unit 5	32	Unit 23	104
Unit 6	36	Unit 24	108
Unit 7	40	Unit 25	112
Unit 8	44	Unit 26	116
Unit 9	48	Unit 27	120
Unit 10	52	Unit 28	124
Unit 11	56	Unit 29	128
Unit 12	60	Unit 30	132
Unit 13	64	Unit 31	136
Unit 14	68	Unit 32	140
Unit 15	72	Unit 33	144
Unit 16	76	Unit 34	148
Unit 17	80	Unit 35	152
Unit 18	84	Unit 36	156

Introduction

This new Reading Comprehension & Writing Skills Program is part of Jolly Literacy and sits alongside the Spelling, Grammar, & Punctuation Program. Reading comprehension and writing skills are natural accompaniments as they allow children to use the knowledge they are being taught in their spelling, grammar, and punctuation lessons, but in an analytical, creative, imaginative, and independent way.

What is Jolly Literacy?

Jolly Literacy builds on the teaching of Jolly Phonics, a multisensory and active program, which aims to teach young children to read and write by applying the English alphabetic code and the five key skills:

1. Learning the letter sounds
2. Learning letter formation
3. Blending (for reading)
4. Identifying the sounds in words (for writing)
5. Tricky words

Following on from Jolly Phonics, Jolly Literacy will offer two, six-level programs that work together seamlessly to give children the skills they need to refine their spelling and punctuation, expand their vocabulary, and develop their reading comprehension and writing skills. They should have a clearer understanding of how language works while becoming confident readers and enthusiastic writers:

Spelling, Grammar, & Punctuation provides two lessons a week. It teaches new spelling patterns, dictionary and thesaurus skills, an understanding of sentence structure, and complex grammatical concepts in an engaging and child-friendly way. The systematic and cumulative syllabus encourages children to spell and punctuate more accurately, use a wider vocabulary, and develop insights into how language works. Its structured approach is suited to whole-school, whole-class teaching but it also works well with individual children.

Reading Comprehension & Writing Skills provides two further weekly lessons. In the first, the children explore, read, and analyze a variety of rich, interesting texts that reinforce and utilize the spelling and vocabulary that have been taught. The second lesson uses those texts as a springboard for stimulating ideas that not only promote creative, imaginative, and independent writing, but also reflect and employ the grammar and punctuation they have learned.

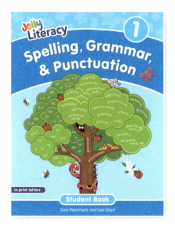
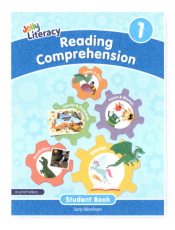
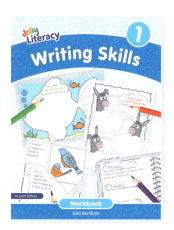

This leaves a day free for teachers to focus on other literacy work, such as group and individual reading or handwriting practice. It is important to show the children how their spelling and grammar work relates to these areas. For instance, if they have recently learned about compound words and there is an example of one in the poem they are reading, the children should be encouraged to look for it.

3

PART 1: Introduction

Introduction

How does Jolly Literacy link to TEFL?

Teaching both programs across the week enables children to develop effective communication skills, helping them express themselves accurately and confidently in English. This is a lifelong skill and is necessary for children to begin to develop intellectually, socially, emotionally, culturally, and spiritually.

The focus of Jolly Literacy progressively develops reading comprehension and writing skills, which are the foundation for the English level exams, and provides additional opportunities to practice speaking and using vocabulary and language structures.

Together, the programs offer a complete foundation for English language learning, using topics and themes that allow for vocabulary acquisition, as well as scaffolding more complex concepts of English that are introduced in later levels.

What is in the Reading Comprehension & Writing Skills Program?

- a complete, structured program from Levels 1–6 (for children aged 5 – 11)
- each level contains 36 weeks of unique comprehension and writing units—one lesson of Reading Comprehension and one lesson of Writing Skills per unit
- an hour for each lesson, dependent on usage, but also with the flexibility to be used in different ways in a variety of settings
- full-color, write-in **Reading Comprehension Student Book** featuring the text to read and activities to complete
- black and white, write-in **Writing Skills Workbook** to support independent writing
- full-color Teacher's Book containing step-by-step lesson plans, further activities and extension ideas

For each level, a copy of the appropriate **Reading Comprehension Student Book** should be given to every student in the class. For ease of use, the **Teacher's Book** has a comprehensive introduction to the program and explains the methodology—it is a good idea to read this before starting the Program. The second part of the **Teacher's Book** provides structured lesson plans that give step-by-step guidance on all aspects of both the Reading Comprehension and the Writing Skills lesson, including the **Student Book** activities. For each unit, the first spread covers Reading Comprehension; the second spread deals with Writing Skills.

How should the core materials be used?

Reading Comprehension Student Book:

Each unit in the **Student Book** features a piece of text to read together, which reflects the topics of the Spelling, Grammar, & Punctuation teaching of that week. A variety of different genres are included from stories to rhymes, plays, fact files, diary entries, and postcards with an engaging mix of photographic images and illustrations. Alongside the text are purposeful questions and activities requiring children to understand and reflect on what they have heard or read. The write-in element of the **Student Book** allows the child real ownership of their learning journey, as they interact with the text, discuss questions, write answers, and gain deeper insights into what they have read. Giving each child their own **Student Book** also makes it easier for teachers to assess the children's answers and penmanship as they strive toward the learning objectives.

Introduction

Writing Skills Workbook:

The **Writing Skills Workbook** enables children to develop their own independent, imaginative, and creative ideas around the topic taught for that week. There are options for illustrating their own writing, pages and objects to cut out and use, decorative frames for stories, fun shapes to write in, and interesting lined layouts to shape and support their writing. Children will be challenged and inspired to take a turn at creating their own range of texts—from poems, stories, invitations, recipes, and newspaper reports.

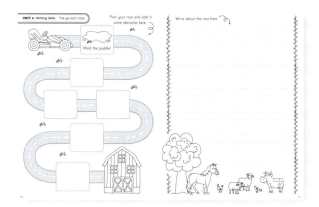 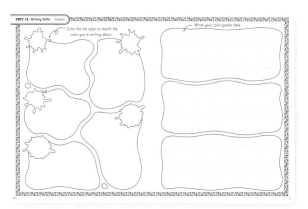

Teacher Book:

The **Reading Comprehension & Writing Skills Teacher's Book** is the essential teaching resource for the program, providing step-by-step plans for both the reading comprehension and writing lessons. The easily navigable book pulls together all the elements to talk about and discuss with the class, suggests books and stories to extend reading, gives rhyme time options, provides extensions for higher level students, and adds further activities to try around the unit.

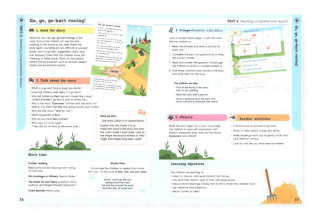 

Texts/formats covered in Level 1:

• Story (fiction)	• Postcard	• Fable	• Newspaper report
• Poem	• Diary	• Folktale	• Recipe
• Rhyme	• Play	• Nonfiction	

Introduction

Example of unit structure in Level 1:

Spelling practiced:	<qu>
Spelling list/recap:	on; but; plum; quick; quiz; queen; squid; to; do; squirrel
Grammar lesson:	proper nouns
Reading Comprehension lesson:	a postcard about an Australian animal park
Writing Skills lesson:	writing and addressing a postcard

Why is reading comprehension important?

Reading is a necessary and lifelong skill for a child to have with the two components, language comprehension and word reading, working in tandem together.

Language comprehension begins at birth and is developed as adults talk to children—chattering about their routine and the world around them. This awareness broadens as carers use stories, nonfiction, and rhymes to introduce children to a wide range of words and their meanings. Words that they may not have used or heard often are introduced through listening to stories and other forms of text, and this increases a child's vocabulary, improves their knowledge of different concepts, and solidifies their understanding.

Word reading is taught later and requires both the pronunciation of unfamiliar words (decoding) and the understanding and recognition of familiar printed words. Underpinning both is the knowledge that the letters on the page represent the sounds of the spoken words.

Reading comprehension therefore unites a child's linguistic knowledge with their awareness and understanding of the world around them. It's essential that children are encouraged to explore a wide range of texts, to read widely, feed their imagination, and discuss their thoughts with other people. When children fully understand what they are reading and can articulate their thinking effectively, they increase their opportunities to develop culturally, emotionally, intellectually, socially, and spiritually.

Oral development

The importance of spoken language in a young child's development cannot be underestimated. Not only is the quality and variety of language heard by children essential for the improvement of their vocabulary and grammar and for their understanding of reading and writing, but being able to verbalize and discuss their own ideas is vital. A child's confidence grows when they feel able to share their thoughts in class, explain their understanding of what they have read, and put forward their opinion for debate. It also allows them to fully prepare their ideas before they begin writing.

Introduction

A note about story time

Reading books to children is enormously important and develops their vocabulary, comprehension, and general knowledge of the world. Sadly, time to read stories in schools is something that is often sacrificed due to time constraints and for other 'more important' aspects of the English curriculum. It is not envisaged that the entire story time panel become part of the comprehension lesson, but the suggestions are there to encourage finding time, perhaps 10-15 minutes several times a week, to share books and stories.

The books should not just be read aloud by the teacher, while the children simply listen. They should be shared and discussed, with both the text and illustrations being considered. After a page has been read—hopefully with expression and using different voices for different characters—the page and pictures can be shown. The teacher should then explain any difficult words or concepts, before asking the children some questions. Different types of questions should be used to check comprehension, to help children develop an understanding of inference, to encourage the children to think about what they have read, and to develop their own opinions.

Included within the story time panel are other ways of enjoying and sharing language, with songs, rhymes, and even jokes. Rhymes are something children enjoy listening to and saying but can become neglected in many school environments. Rhymes, songs, and poems support phonological awareness and provide fun ways to engage with and play with language, rhyme, rhythm, and alliteration. They are also a great way of developing memory. For children learning English as an additional language, rhymes can help with accent and with the cadences of spoken English. Rhymes can also provide an opportunity for sharing with family members—to talk and learn about favorite rhymes from their parents' or grandparents' childhoods and/or from different cultures.

One of the most important reasons rhymes are included in the program is that they offer children an opportunity to speak in front of others in a fun and unstressful way. Again, it is not envisaged that this is done entirely within the comprehension lesson. While the rhyme, poem, or song can be introduced within the lesson, the children can be encouraged to learn it at home. Individuals, pairs, or groups of children, as appropriate, can then recite the rhyme to the rest of the class at times during the week—perhaps before going to recess or lunch. Speaking in a group can support a child who is not a confident speaker, and hopefully eventually give them the confidence to speak on their own.

How do the comprehension units work within the program?

The reading comprehension units in the Reading Comprehension & Writing Skills Program provide opportunities for children to spend time analyzing different types of text. The teacher is asked to read the text with the class initially and to point out any words the children may need explaining. Doing this allows the children to weave the meaning of the new words into a context that makes sense to them and contributes to developing their early skills of inference. They may look at, and talk about, the punctuation, the sentence structure, and revisit the spelling and grammar learning from the week too.

Next, there is discussion about the meaning of the text. The specific questions given in the **Teacher's Book** will prompt plenty of opportunities for children to share their answers, discuss thoughts with others, and ask questions of their own. Some of the questions in the **Teacher's Book** are deliberately open-ended and may elicit an emotional response from the children as they are asked to share their opinion and draw on their own knowledge.

The focus then turns to the written activities contained in the **Reading Comprehension Student Book**. Children are asked to read a short phrase from the text and then draw a picture to show they have understood what that phrase means. They complete "yes" and "no" questions, which may require revisiting the text with either their teacher or in a group. They then read some short questions and write answers, the details for which can be found within the text but may be discussed as a class prior to this. For children who require a further challenge, there are other suggested activities they may also like to try.

Coming together as a plenary to reread the text is vital. The teacher may choose different children, groups, or the whole class to read sections or the entire text. Listening to others read, concentrating on reading aloud with

Introduction

expression and fluency, and participating fully in sharing this class activity, builds confidence and allows children to begin to understand how language can be structured and interpreted in different ways.

What does the Science of Reading say about comprehension?

The Science of Reading is a term that encapsulates all the evidence-aligned research compiled over the last fifty years, which shows us how students master reading and writing skills. Linguists, cognitive psychologists, neuroscientists, and other specialists across many nations, languages, and disciplines have concluded that to create competent readers and writers we must understand how these skills develop in the brain and teach and assess our students accordingly.

Reading Comprehension is both a product and a process, as Gough and Tumner's *Simple View of Reading* (1986) explains:

$$WR \times LC = RC$$

To be a competent reader, a student must have both accurate and automatic Word Recognition (WR – the ability to lift the word off the page) and Language Comprehension (LC—the ability to understand the meaning of spoken/signed language). The two elements interact and influence each other, and both are required and practiced in the reading and comprehension of this Program.

Why are writing skills important?

Children need to learn how to write accurately and legibly in order to communicate and express themselves. As with reading, there are two components that need to develop in tandem—transcription (spelling and handwriting) and composition (articulating ideas and structuring them in speech, then writing).

Transcription relies on the ability of children to spell quickly and accurately, with a firm understanding of the relationship between sounds and letters, as well as an increasing awareness of word structure. At the start of Level 1, children will often still be spelling words in a phonically plausible way, so modeling new words and providing opportunities for children to practice writing new vocabulary is essential.

Composition is a cognitive process—a great deal of thinking needs to go on before children can even begin to start expressing themselves in a clear, coherent, and organized way. By talking about what they are going to write about, and composing their thoughts orally before they start writing, children are better able to clarify their ideas and check that their meaning is clear.

Giving children plenty of opportunities to practice their own writing, as well as modeling writing for them to follow, supports children in both their transcription and composition, and allows them to begin to see language patterns. As they are shown their ideas in writing, they can link the sounds they know to actual words and real meaning. Gradually they will become aware of the audience they are writing for, understand the purpose and context for which they are writing, and learn to weave in new vocabulary and grammar.

How do the writing units work within the program?

The writing skills units in the Reading Comprehension & Writing Skills Program aim to support children as they explore their own ideas and find ways to communicate those thoughts. In the introductory activity, the teacher is asked to remind the children of the text they heard or read during the comprehension lesson, and then open a discussion on the topic of that piece of writing. The class may be asked to recall their favorite bits of the writing or share an opinion or experience related to the topic.

The explanation that comes next in the **Teacher's Book**, breaks apart the text and allows the teacher the opportunity to ask the children specific questions, which will help them to formulate their own writing. The teacher may ask about the format or style of the text, its structure, and the grammar points it covers. Discussing the concepts covered in the text will help the children begin to think about, verbalize, and draft their own ideas.

Following this, the teacher talks through the step-by-step instructions for the writing activity. At this point, the class can either make use of the **Writing Skills Workbook**, which is designed to provide a supportive, engaging environment

Introduction

for the children to try out their writing, or use their own lined exercise books.

Working on their own writing, children may begin by composing their sentences orally, by creating a visual plan, by copying the modeled writing from the teacher, or by organizing their thoughts in pictures before they begin to write. The **Writing Skills Workbook** encourages and provides this planning space, while the Teacher's Book describes these steps in detail.

As with the Reading Comprehension units, coming together for plenary allows a recap for both the children and the teacher. Asking children to read aloud and share their work is a great way for the class to check the accuracy of their own writing and to hear other children's interpretation of the activity.

What is the Science of Writing?

Although not as extensively researched over the years as the Science of Reading, it is important, as part of all literacy studies, to address the research on writing too.

"The body of research is substantial in both number of studies and quality of studies. There's no question that reading and writing share a lot of real estate, they depend on a lot of the same knowledge and skills"—Timothy Shanahan, Emeritus Professor of Education, University of Illinois, Chicago.

Both forms of communication deepen the children's background knowledge, vocabulary, text knowledge, and understanding of inference and metaphor. Research on explicit, evidence-based writing instruction has also shown that this, in turn, will increase a reader's fluency and reading comprehension. The structured approach of this Reading Comprehension & Writing Skills Program guides the student into the basics of good sentence structure and different elements of various genres, syntax, and semantics, while giving them the scope to develop their own ideas and discover new interests and skills.

Learning Objectives for Year 1

In order to complete the reading comprehension and writing skills activities, the units are written in such a way that they require the children to listen to, talk about, and recall details of the text being shared with them. Open-ended questions and class discussion prompt children to extrapolate what they need from the text to answer questions, as well as to link what they hear or read to their own experiences.

In every unit, children are given opportunities to discuss word meanings, link new words to those they already know, and talk about the different features of a text. Through the progression of the units, children become familiar with, and can retell, traditional stories, and start to use inference and prediction as they gain confidence.

The addition of rhyme time within each lesson provides a platform for an appreciation of songs, rhymes, and poems, as the children are encouraged to say these aloud with the teacher and recite them by heart (either individually or in groups). Confidence in speaking aloud and the ability to listen to others are vital skills to have.

Being able to talk about what they will write about, plan aloud, and use plans or pictures to support their thoughts helps children make use of new vocabulary in their writing, formulate their sentences effectively, aids their memory, and gives shape to their creative ideas. At this level, children will trial new words with phonically plausible spellings, but encouraging them to re-read their work, check for accuracy, and even read aloud is best practice for the future.

Help for struggling students

Throughout the Reading Comprehension & Writing Skills Program the importance of planning (both orally and on paper) and the use of illustrations and pictures to support children's writing have been emphasized. For struggling students, or students with SEN, these supports are vital for success.

Allowing children who are experiencing difficulties in expressing themselves to draw or illustrate their contributions, offers them an initial outlet to begin the writing process. For this reason, the **Writing Skills Workbook** provides visual prompts, illustrations, and writing frames to color, segregated areas that represent where to write the beginning, middle, and end of a story, and dedicated pages for planning and story maps.

Writing assignments can seem very overwhelming for children who aren't helped to see the piece of work in smaller steps, so breaking down tasks into more manageable elements is also essential. While the **Reading Comprehension & Writing Skills Teacher's Book**

Introduction

provides steps to work through, breaking these down further—focusing more time on just one element, limiting the number of questions or activities, and asking the children to answer orally instead of on paper—could all help in developing and organizing children's thoughts.

In some cases, children may not be able to pick up on the teacher's intended instruction or be confident enough or ready to work on their own. Arranging for children to work in small groups or pairings, thereby providing a struggling child with a talking buddy, also allows children to formulate their ideas together before they begin their own writing.

Further accommodations could include:

- providing graphic organizers (concept/story maps)
- offering extended writing prompts
- altering the size or amount of writing paper or writing tools
- using alternative means to record ideas—some children may require a scribe to write for them or use an augmentative device or predictive text computer program
- modeling expectations, especially for those students with visual processing difficulties

Supplementary materials

Many of the other materials published by Jolly can be used in conjunction with the Reading Comprehension & Writing Skills Program:

- **Jolly Dictionary** encourages children to become independent learners by looking up words to check meaning and spelling.
- **Jolly Plays** not only provide valuable reading, speaking, and listening practice, but also include comprehension questions, discussion topics, cross-curricular activities, and writing activities.
- **Jolly Phonics Readers** (Blue and Purple Level—Inky, Snake, and Bee; General Fiction; Nonfiction; Our World Readers; and Folk Tales) make good additions for further independent reading, as the phonic knowledge required for the Program is the same as the Purple Level Readers.
- **Jolly Phonics Alphabet and Alternative Spelling Posters** and **Jolly Phonic Tricky Word Wall Flowers** will both help children quickly recall the alphabet, capital letter formation, main alternative spellings, and tricky word spellings.
- The **Jolly Phonics Handwriting Books** are ideal for children who require extra letter-formation practice. A set of seven small books cover the lower-case letters and digraphs, and a larger book focuses on the capital letters and their sounds.

Reading Comprehension lesson

How to navigate a Reading Comprehension lesson in the **Student Book**:

The unit number and type of lesson.

The genre, or type, of writing used in the lesson.

This activity allows children to show they understand what they are reading by drawing something to illustrate the writing. It is also an opportunity to reinforce correct pencil grip and aid fine motor control.

Text for reading together, for discussion and to analyze. Carefully selected words have been used to practice the spellings, tricky words and grammar taught during the week. An opportunity to highlight and practice learning from previous lessons too.

Children need to read the sentence and decide if it is right or wrong, then circle "yes" or "no" accordingly. Answers can often be found in the text, so the text may need to be reread and discussed.

This written answer activity requires children to write in a complete sentence, where appropriate. An opportunity to check letter formation and spacing, as well as the accuracy of answers.

On occasions, answers do not need to be in full sentences, but letter formation and accuracy should still be maintained.

How to navigate a Reading Comprehension lesson in the **Teacher's Book**:

The unit number and type of lesson to be taught can be found on these tabs throughout the Teacher's Book.

Title of the lesson.

The Student Book page containing the Reading Comprehension text is added here for easy reference.

Step 3 provides guidance on how the children can complete the activity page linked to the text.

The Student Book page containing the activities is added here for easy reference. There are suggested answers provided as guidance.

Step-by-step guidelines provide instructions for each part of the lesson. Step 1 is to read the text through—with the children able to hear and see the words clearly.

Step 2 is essential for the children to discuss their thoughts, ask and answer questions, and share their opinions.

Anything that needs explaining or discussing in depth is highlighted in panels.

Here are suggestions for further reading. It is important to read and share stories together. It provides children with the opportunity to discuss vocabulary and talk about what they are reading, therefore helping to develop their comprehension. Reading books allows children to explore the subject and the world beyond their immediate environment.

This is an opportunity for children to learn or recite rhymes/text, either individually or together. Having the confidence to speak in front of other people is a valuable skill.

The Learning Objectives list the skills or knowledge that are covered in each lesson.

Some suggestions of further activities connected to the things the children are learning in the unit.

Linked to the topic, these extension activities can be done as a class, individually, or tried in groups.

Step 4 brings the class together in order to read the text again. This is an opportunity for the children to read and listen to each other as a group.

PART 1: Introduction

11

Writing Skills lesson

PART 1: Introduction

How to navigate a Writing Skills lesson in the **Workbook**:

- The unit number and type of lesson.
- Most instructions can be found in the Teacher's Book, but there may be labels to help guide the children too.
- The children are encouraged to think about and plan what they are going to write and make decisions on how to color or illustrate their work.
- Lined space is provided for the children's writing. It can help them focus on their ideas, presentation, and to be proud of their writing.

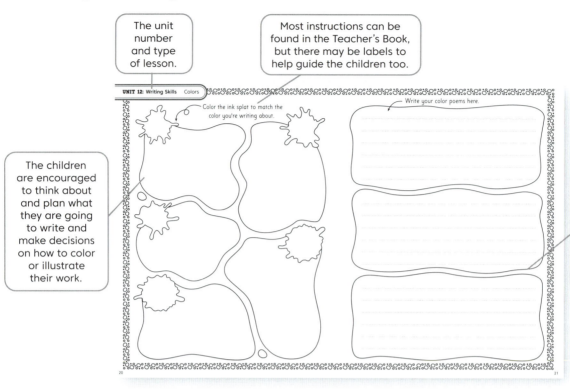

How to navigate a Writing Skills lesson in the **Teacher's Book**:

- Step-by-step guidelines provide instructions for each part of the lesson. Step 1 may be to remind the children about the topic they discussed in the Reading Comprehension lesson, reread the text, or revisit vocabulary.
- The unit number and type of lesson to be taught can be found on these tabs throughout the Teacher's Book.
- This is the title of the lesson.
- Step 4 brings the class together so the children can share their work, as well as read and listen to each other as a group.
- Linked to the topic, these extension activities can be done as a class, individually, or tried in groups.
- Step 2 allows the children to discuss their thoughts, ask and answer questions, and share their opinions. They will often begin to plan their writing out loud at this stage.
- The assessment criteria is graduated in order for the teacher to quickly assess the ability of each child based on the work for that unit and give feedback where needed.
- Step 3 provides guidance on the writing the children will be doing.
- Often the Workbook page will be shown here for planning purposes and easy reference.
- Some suggestions of further activities connected to the things the children are learning in the unit.
- Anything that needs explaining or discussing in depth is highlighted in panels.
- The Learning Objectives list the skills or knowledge that are covered in each lesson.

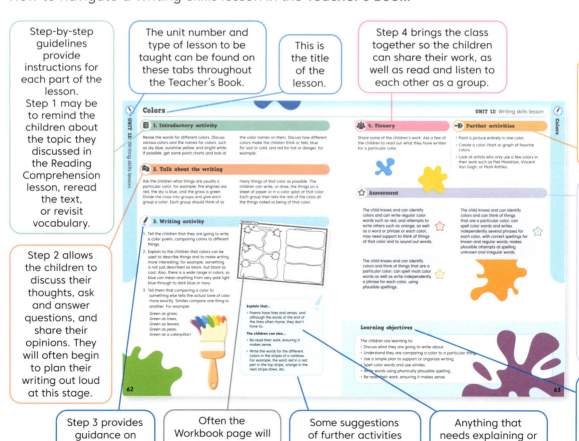

12

Scope & Sequence Level 1: Weeks 1 to 12

	Week 1	Week 2	Week 3	Week 4	Week 5	Week 6	Week 7	Week 8	Week 9	Week 10	Week 11	Week 12
Spelling Patterns			Jolly Phonics digraphs				short vowels	short vowels & consonant doubling			/air/ spellings	
	<sh>	<ch>	<th>	<ng>	<qu>	<ar>	short vowels	<ff>, <ll>, <ss>, <zz>	<ck>	<air>	<ear>	<are>
	• Reinforce and extend the children's phonic knowledge in the weekly spelling lessons with spelling lists, word banks, dictation, and spelling tests. • Develop the children's writing skills: segment spelling list words and use "chin bumps" for longer words; write words/sentences from dictation; use words with focus graphemes in sentences. • Provide systematic revision using flashcards, the short vowel actions, the vowel hand, and the vowels song.											
Tricky Words			set 1						set 2			
	I the	he she	me we	be was	to do	are all	you your	come some	said here	there they	go no	so my
	• Revise the 72 tricky words taught in Jolly Phonics, ensuring the tricky parts are known and can be recognized (for reading) and remembered (for writing). • Use familiar spelling strategies like saying it as it sounds, mnemonics, and the tricky word spelling routine to help the children remember the tricky parts. • Practice writing the tricky words regularly in the weekly spelling tests and sentence dictation. • Use flashcards/the tricky word wall display for regular reading practice. Introduce the Jolly Phonics Readers, Purple Level to confident readers who have finished the Blue Level.											
Spelling, Grammar, & Punctuation						initial consonant blends						
	<cl->	<bl->	<fl->	<gl->	<pl->	<sl->	<br->	<cr->	<dr->	<fr->	<gr->	<pr->
	• Practice initial consonant blends regularly to help the children blend fluently and spell unfamiliar words accurately, using flashcards, dictation, blends wheels, and the spelling lists.											
	capitals	sentences		upper and lower case matching			alphabetical order	a / an	plurals <-s>	plurals <-es>		initial blends
	• Point out examples in the texts the children are reading where spelling, grammar, or vocabulary points overlap, such as the use of "an" before words starting with a vowel sound.											
Parts of Speech						nouns		articles		plural nouns	pronouns	
						proper common		a / an	<-s>	<-es> singular and plural	personal	
						a capital letter for proper nouns						
	• Introduce the parts of speech using simple definitions that expand over time, along with a color and action. • Only concrete nouns, personal pronouns, and simple tenses are introduced in Level 1.											
Reading Comprehension & Writing Skills	A visit to the aquarium (story)	A day at the beach (story)	The three donkeys (story)	Animal alphabet (poem)	An Australian animal park (postcard)	Go, go, go-kart racing! (story)	My week (diary)	Puffins (nonfiction)	Hickory dickory dock (rhyme)	The Wind and the Sun (play)	The Wind and the Sun (fable)	Flower Farm (story)
	Writing full sentences	Retelling a story	Filling in thought bubbles	Creating an alliterative poem	Writing and addressing a postcard	Describing a go-kart race	Recording a week in diary entries	Creating a fact file	Making rhyming sentences	Performing a play	Retelling a fable	Writing a color poem
	• Reinforce the children's understanding of basic sentence structure in their reading and writing—begin with a simple definition and expand over time. • Encourage the children to use techniques like finger spaces to make sure words are separated clearly in their writing.											

PART 2: Scope & Sequence

PART 2: Scope & Sequence

Scope & Sequence Level 1: Weeks 13 to 24

	Week 13	Week 14	Week 15	Week 16	Week 17	Week 18	Week 19	Week 20	Week 21	Week 22	Week 23	Week 24
Spelling Patterns	<y> as /ee/	long vowels & magic <e> — hop-over <e> digraphs		<ear> as /ear/	<ph>	<wh>	<ay>	<ea>	<igh>	<y> as /ie/	<ow> as /oa/	<ew>
	• Reinforce and extend the children's phonic knowledge in the weekly spelling lessons with spelling lists, word banks, dictation, and spelling tests. • Develop the children's writing skills: segment spelling list words and use "chin bumps" for longer words; write words/sentences from dictation; use words with focus graphemes in sentences. • Provide systematic revision using flashcards, the short vowel actions, the vowel hand, and the vowels song.											
Tricky Words	one by	only old	like have	live give	little down	what when	why where	who which	any many	more before	other were	because want
	set 3								set 4			
	• Revise the 72 tricky words taught in Jolly Phonics, ensuring the tricky parts are known and can be recognized (for reading) and remembered (for writing). • Use familiar spelling strategies like say it as it sounds, mnemonics, and the tricky word spelling routine to help the children remember the tricky parts. • Practice writing the tricky words regularly in the weekly spelling tests and sentence dictation. • Use flashcards/the tricky word wall display for regular reading practice. Introduce the Jolly Phonics Readers, Purple Level to confident readers who have finished the Blue Level.											
Spelling, Grammar, & Punctuation	initial consonant blends								final consonant blends			
	<tr->	<sc->	<sm->	<sn->	<sw->	<tw->	<sk->	<sp->	<-nt>	<-st>	<-lb>	<-ld>
	• Practice initial consonant blends regularly to help the children blend fluently and spell unfamiliar words accurately, using flashcards, dictation, blends wheels, and the spelling lists.										final blends	compound words
			verbs <-es>	tenses: past <-ed>	doubling rule		joining words and phrases with "and"					
			conjugation	regular verbs								
	verbs	**verbs & pronouns**			**past tense**	**verbs: future**						
	present tense			<-ed>	doubling rule	shall / will						
Parts of Speech									**nouns**	**adjectives**		
									common & proper	positives	comps & sups	
	• Point out examples in the texts the children are reading where spelling, grammar, or vocabulary points overlap, such as the use of "an" before words starting with a vowel sound. • Introduce the parts of speech using simple, child-friendly definitions that expand over time, along with a color and action. • Practice simple parsing activities regularly, identifying one or more parts of speech in sentences by underlining the words in the appropriate color/doing the action. • Only concrete nouns, personal pronouns, and simple tenses are introduced in Level 1.									parse the PoS in sentences		
Reading Comprehension & Writing Skills	Grandpa's party (story)	A thank-you cake (story)	Anansi the spider and the melon (folktale)	Globes (nonfiction)	Boat trip (story)	How the whale got his throat (fable)	Book Week (story)	Characters (story)	The night sky (story)	Monster party (story)	The abominable snowman (story)	Monster Times (newspaper report)
	Creating an invitation	Compiling a recipe	Retelling a story	Describing a creature	Composing an acrostic poem	Writing about the future	Creating a book cover	Describing a story character	Writing about themselves	Describing a monster	Recording a meeting of monsters	Compiling a news report
	• Reinforce the children's understanding of basic sentence structure (first introduced in Jolly Phonics) in their reading and writing. • Begin with a simple, child-friendly definition and expand it over time: Sentences start with a capital letter, end with a period, and make sense. • Encourage the children to use techniques like finger spaces to make sure words are separated clearly in their writing.											

Scope & Sequence Level 1: Weeks 25 to 36

	Week 25	Week 26	Week 27	Week 28	Week 29	Week 30	Week 31	Week 32	Week 33	Week 34	Week 35	Week 36
Spelling Patterns	alternative spellings of other vowels							alternative spellings of other vowels				
	‹ou›	‹ow› as /ou/	‹oi›	‹oy›	‹or›	‹al›	‹nk› as /ng-k/	‹er›	‹ir›	‹ur›	‹au›	‹aw›
	• Reinforce and extend the children's phonic knowledge in the weekly spelling lessons with spelling lists, word banks, dictation, and spelling tests. • Develop the children's writing skills: segment spelling list words and use "chin bumps" for longer words; write words/sentences from dictation; use words with focus graphemes in sentences. • Provide systematic revision using flashcards, the short vowel actions, the vowel hand, and the vowels song.											
Tricky Words			set 5						set 6			
	saw put	could should	would right	two four	goes does	made their	once upon	always also	of eight	love cover	after every	mother father
	• Revise the 72 tricky words taught in Jolly Phonics, ensuring the tricky parts are known and can be recognized (for reading) and remembered (for writing). • Use familiar spelling strategies like say it as it sounds, mnemonics, and the tricky word spelling routine to help the children remember the tricky parts. • Practice writing the tricky words regularly in the weekly spelling tests and sentence dictation. • Use flashcards/the tricky word wall display for regular reading practice.											
Spelling, Grammar, & Punctuation						final consonant blends						
	‹-lf›	‹-lk›	‹-lm›	‹-lp›	‹-lt›	‹-ct›	‹-ft›	‹-nt›	‹-pt›	‹-xt›	‹-mp›	‹-nd›
	• Practice initial consonant blends regularly to help the children blend fluently and spell unfamiliar words accurately, using flashcards, dictation, blends wheels, and the spelling lists.											
	sentence sequencing			suffixes	use "and" to join sentences	antonyms / ‹un-›	using a dictionary	speech marks	word webs	questions words & question marks	parsing	parsing
	• Point out examples in the texts the children are reading where spelling, grammar, or vocabulary points overlap, such as the use of "an" before words starting with a vowel sound.											
Parts of Speech		verbs	adverbs									parsing a story
		identify the verbs and adverbs in sentences										
	• Introduce the parts of speech using simple, child-friendly definitions that expand over time, along with a color and action. • Practice simple parsing activities regularly, identifying one, or more parts of speech in sentences by underlining the words in the appropriate color/doing the action. • Only concrete nouns, personal pronouns, and simple tenses are introduced in Level 1.											
Reading Comprehension & Writing Skills	Cloud watching (story)	Monsters verbs (rhyme)	The chatty tortoise (fable)	My best toy (story)	Once Upon a Time Street (story)	Jack and the Beanstalk (story)	Alice down the rabbit hole (story)	Animal chatter (poem)	Bird spotting (story)	The enormous turnip (fable)	Dinosaur names (nonfiction)	Strawberry sundae (recipe)
	Creating an acrostic poem	Composing rhymes	Retelling a fable	Writing an imaginative story	Focusing on a character	Continuing a story	Retelling and adding to a story	Compiling an animal poem	Using alternative words	Creating a new version of a fable	Describing a dinosaur	Creating a recipe
	• Reinforce the children's understanding of basic sentence structure (first introduced in Jolly Phonics) in their reading and writing. • Begin with a simple, child-friendly definition and expand it over time: Sentences start with a capital letter, end with a period, and make sense. • Encourage the children to use techniques like finger spaces to make sure words are separated clearly in their writing.											

PART 2: Scope & Sequence

UNIT 1: Reading comprehension lesson

A visit to the aquarium

 ## 1. Read the story

Read the story to the class. Ensure the children can see the text, pointing to the words as you read. Read the story again, sounding out any difficult or unusual words, such as *aquarium* and *shoal*. Check that the children know the meaning of these words. Briefly look at the punctuation: mention the speech marks and explain that the words inside them are the words that are actually said, and point out the exclamation point following *Wow!*

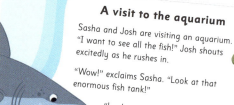

A visit to the aquarium

Sasha and Josh are visiting an aquarium. "I want to see all the fish!" Josh shouts excitedly as he rushes in.

"Wow!" exclaims Sasha. "Look at that enormous fish tank!"

"Look at all the different fish," Josh whispers.

"I can see a shoal of red fish," says Sasha.

"I wish we could swim in there," says Josh.

Just then a big shark swims out of the shadows and across the tank. "Perhaps not," mutters Josh with a shiver.

Finally, they do some shopping. Sasha chooses a bag of shells and Josh gets a toy shark.

"He's fin-tastic," says Josh, cuddling his shark and smiling happily.

2. Talk about the story

- What is an aquarium?
- What are the names of the children?
- Why don't they see the shark to begin with?
- Why do you think Josh does not want to swim in the tank after all?
- What do they buy?
- Why does Josh say *fin-tastic*?
- How do you know Josh is having a good time?
- Why do you think they are visiting the aquarium? *(They like fish or they are on a day trip.)*

Point out that...

The plural (meaning there is more than one of them) of fish can be *fish* or *fishes*, as in the title of one of the books suggested below. *Fishes* often refers to lots of different types or species of fish.

Story time

Further reading

Read some stories about fish, for example:

The Rainbow Fish Marcus Pfister

Kate and the Fishes Kayley Turner (author) and MBE Studioz (illustrator)

Hooray for Fish! Lucy Cousins

Rhyme time

Encourage the children to sing this song with you to the tune of **The wheels on the bus**:

The teeth on a shark are sharp, sharp, sharp,
Sharp, sharp, sharp,
Sharp, sharp, sharp.
The teeth on a shark are sharp, sharp, sharp.
Snap! Snap! Snap!

16

UNIT 1: Reading comprehension lesson

3. Comprehension activities

Look at Student Book page 3 with the class. Tell the children to:

1. Read the phrases and draw a picture for each one.
2. Complete the yes / no questions by circling the correct answer.
3. Read and answer the question. Encourage the children to write a complete sentence.

> **The children can also...**
> - Find all the words in the story with a <sh> spelling.
> - Read the story with a partner.
> - Write a sentence from the story and draw a picture to illustrate their words.

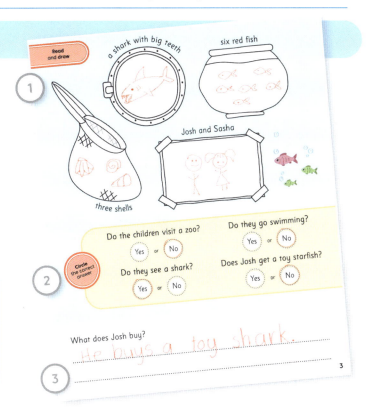

4. Plenary

Read the story again as a class. Encourage the children to use the punctuation to help them read with expression and fluency.

Further activities

- Create wax-resist aquarium pictures. Draw an aquarium scene on a rectangular sheet of white paper using wax crayons. Mix blue paint and water to get a very watery paint and brush this lightly over the wax-crayon picture.

- Draw, paint, or make some collaged fish, which can be real or imaginary. An aquarium display could then be made by the whole class.
- The children can make a display of books about fish that they find in the library.

Learning objectives

- The children are learning to:
- Listen to, discuss, and recall details from story texts.
- Link what they hear to their own experiences.
- Discuss word meanings, linking new words to those they already know.
- Use inference and prediction.
- Recite rhymes by heart.

A visit to the aquarium

17

Fishy tales

UNIT 1: Writing skills lesson

1. Introductory activity

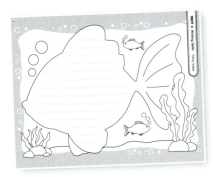

This piece of free writing enables an assessment of the children's ability at the start of the year.

Remind the children about the story **A visit to the aquarium**. Briefly discuss what the class knows about fish. Ask if any of the children have been to an aquarium or a sealife center and what they saw and did there.

Remind the children to listen to others when they are speaking and to wait their turn to speak.

2. Talk about the writing

Retell the story of **A visit to the aquarium**. Ask the children what happened at the beginning, middle, and end of the story. Encourage them to answer in sentences. Ask the children some open questions about their own experiences to encourage them to add more detail to their own writing.

Example questions
- Why were the children visiting the aquarium?
- How did the children feel?
- What other fish or creatures might they have seen?

3. Writing activity

1. Ask some of the children to say one sentence from the story. Make sure they stop at the end of the sentence rather than adding, 'and this... and that...'.

   Show the children how to put a finger on their pursed lips to mark the end of a sentence, and remind the children that this is where the period goes.

2. Sound out any difficult words, explain any unusual spellings, and talk about any tricky words as necessary. Some of these words can be written on the board.

3. Ask for some suggestions for a sentence to begin the story. Choose one of the sentences and model it by writing it on the board.

   Remind the children that a sentence starts with a capital letter and ends with a period (or another punctuation mark such as an exclamation point). Remind them to leave spaces between words, sound out any difficult words, and talk about any tricky words.

4. The children copy the starting sentence from the board and continue writing the story. Encourage them to add in some of their own details and ideas.

   The children can also...
   - Re-read their work, ensuring it makes sense.
   - Draw a picture to illustrate their story.
   - Share their work with a partner.

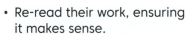

UNIT 1: Writing skills lesson

4. Plenary

Share some of the children's work, either by showing it to the other children or by asking some of them to read out what they have written.

Further activities

- Draw and annotate a fish. Label the eyes, mouth, gills, fin, tail, and scales.
- Watch, and draw, the fish in the school aquarium or from videos on the internet.
- Make a class book or display of the children's pictures and writing.
- Visit the library to find some books on fish.

Assessment

The child writes some words, most of which are plausibly spelled, but uses little or no punctuation.

The child retells the basic story, writing at least half a page independently, and uses some periods and plausible spellings.

The child retells the story in sentences, using information from the text and adding further detail; writes at least one page independently, using periods and correct spelling for most known and regular words; makes plausible attempts at spelling unknown and irregular words.

Also assess handwriting: size, neatness, formation, and joining.

Learning objectives

The children are learning to:
- Listen to, discuss, and recall details from story texts.
- Discuss what they are going to write about.
- Say a sentence.
- Write simple sentences to retell a story.
- Write words using phonically plausible spellings.
- Re-read their writing to check that it makes sense.

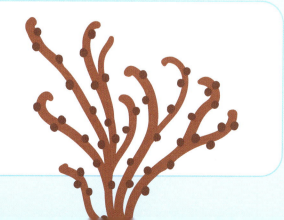

UNIT 2: Reading comprehension lesson

A day at the beach

 1. Read the story

Read the story to the class. Ensure the children can see the text, pointing to the words as you read. Read the story again, sounding out any difficult or unusual words, such as *while*, *sandwiches*, *chocolate*, *huge*, *moat*, and *castle*. Check that the children know the meaning of these words. Point out the capital letters and periods, and briefly indicate the speech marks.

A day at the beach

Charlie and his family are at the beach.

"Let's hunt in the rock pools," suggests Charlie. They see some shrimps, three starfish, and a lot of shells. "Look," Charlie shouts, pointing to some seaweed. "I can see a little crab."

After a while, Charlie says, "I'm hot. Let's go for a swim."

After their swim, the family eat lunch. They have chicken sandwiches, crunchy carrot sticks, and chocolate chip cookies.

Then, the children build a huge sandcastle and decorate it with seashells, stones, seaweed, and some flags that Dad gave them.

Later, they dig a moat around the castle.

"That is such a grand castle," says Dad. "I wonder who lives there?"

 2. Talk about the story

- Where do the family go?
- What is a rock pool?
- What do they see in the rock pools?
- Why does Charlie want to go swimming?
- What do they have for lunch?
- What is a moat?
- Why do castles have moats? *(To deter invaders in the past; for protection.)*
- What might happen to the sandcastle when the tide comes in?
- Who do you think might live in a castle like this?
  (A king or queen; knights; mermaids and mermen.)

Story time

Further reading

Read some stories about a day at the beach, for example:

At the Beach: Postcards from Crabby Spit
Roland Harvey

Ben's Adventures: A Day at the Beach
Elizabeth Gerlach

Day at the Beach
Tom Booth (author and illustrator)

Rhyme time

Say the rhyme with the class. Then, during the week, ask a few children to recite the rhyme together or individually. Encourage them to use the actions of moving their hand in a wave pattern for the word *sea* and putting a hand above their eyes for the word *see*.

*A sailor went to sea, sea, sea,
To see what he could see, see, see,
But all that he could see, see, see,
Was the bottom of the deep blue sea, sea, sea.*

UNIT 2: Reading comprehension lesson

3. Comprehension activities

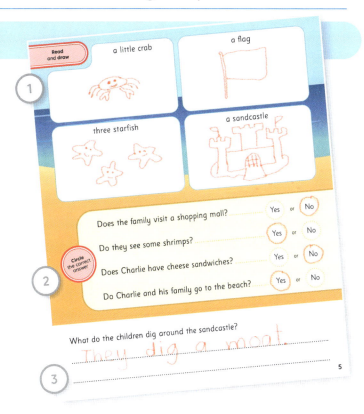

Look at Student Book page 5 with the class. Tell the children to:

1. Read the phrases and draw a picture for each one.
2. Complete the yes / no questions by circling the correct answer.
3. Read and answer the question. Encourage children to write a complete sentence.

> **The children can also...**
> - Find all the words in the story with a <ch> spelling.
> - Read the story with a partner.
> - Write a sentence from the story and draw a picture to illustrate their words.

 ## 4. Plenary

Read the story again as a class. Encourage the children to use the punctuation to help them read with expression and fluency.

Further activities

- Make sandcastles in a sand tray.
- Create a sandcastle collage. Draw a simple castle, add glue, and sprinkle with sand, then decorate with shells.
- Find out about rock pools.
- Talk, or write, about a recent day out.

Learning objectives

The children are learning to:
- Listen to, discuss, and recall details from story texts.
- Link what they hear to their own experiences.
- Discuss word meanings, linking new words to those they already know.
- Use inference and prediction.
- Recite rhymes by heart.

21

At the beach

UNIT 2: Writing skills lesson

Before class
Cut out the pictures in the Student Book on page 75 to use and reorder for this unit.

1. Introductory activities

Briefly discuss what the class knows about beaches. Ask if any of the children have been to a beach and what they saw and did there.

Remind the children to listen to others when they are speaking and to wait their turn to speak.

Include some open questions to encourage the children to add in their own details when they do their writing.

Example questions
- What did they take to the beach?
- What did they do when they arrived?
- What else could they have done?
- Can they describe their sandcastle?

2. Talk about the writing

Re-read the story of **A day at the beach**. Explain that stories have a beginning, a middle—during which various things happen—and an end. Ask the children what happens at the beginning, in the middle, and at the end of this story. Look at the pictures and ask which one comes first in the story. Then ask which ones come in the middle and at the end. Four children could hold a picture each and put themselves in the correct order.

3. Writing activity

1. Arrange the pictures in order on the board.
2. Ask for some suggestions for a sentence to begin the story. (For example: *Charlie and his family went to the beach.*) Make sure the children stop at the end of the sentence rather than adding, 'and this… and that…'.

Show the children how to put a finger on their lips to mark the end of a sentence, and remind the children that this is where the period goes.

3. Choose one of the sentences and model it by writing it on the board. Sound out any difficult words, explain any unusual spellings, and talk about any tricky words.
4. The children copy the starting sentence from the board and continue writing the story. Encourage them to write independently and to try spelling words, even if they are unsure of the correct spelling.

Remind the children that a sentence starts with a capital letter and ends with a period (or another punctuation mark such as a question mark). Remind them to leave spaces between words.

The children can also…
- Re-read their work, ensuring it makes sense.
- Copy the story pictures or draw their own pictures to illustrate their story.
- Share their work with a partner.

UNIT 2: Writing skills lesson

 4. Plenary

Share some of the children's work, either by showing it to the other children or by asking a few of them to read out what they have written.

 Further activities

- Cut up carrot sticks or make sandwiches or chocolate chip cookies.
- Draw a graph of everyone's favorite sandwiches.
- Write about or draw a picture of a recent day trip.

 Assessment

 The child sequences the pictures correctly and says a sentence about each picture; writes some words, most of which are plausibly spelled, but uses little or no punctuation.

 The child sequences the pictures correctly and independently writes two or three sentences about each picture, retelling the basic story and using some periods and plausible spellings.

 The child sequences the pictures correctly and independently writes a few sentences about each picture, with periods, using knowledge from the story and adding extra information; most known andregular words are correctly spelled and phonically plausible attempts are made at unknown and irregular words.

Learning objectives

The children are learning to:
- Listen to, discuss, and recall details from story texts.
- Understand the idea of a story having a beginning, middle, and end.
- Discuss what they are going to write about.
- Say a sentence.
- Write simple sentences to retell a story.
- Re-read their writing to check that it makes sense.
- Write words using phonically plausible spellings.

23

UNIT 3: Reading comprehension lesson

The three donkeys

 1. Read the story

Read the story to the class. Ensure the children can see the text, pointing to the words as you read. Read the story again, sounding out any difficult or unusual words, such as *donkeys*, *thistles,* and *paddock*. Check that the children know the meaning of these words. Ask what they notice about the last sentence, which ends with what looks like several periods (the three dots are called an ellipsis). Explain that the three dots mean that the sentence is not finished and that at the end of the lesson you are going to ask them for ideas about how to finish the sentence.

The three donkeys

Thor, Moth, and Thad are donkeys. They are looking hungrily at a patch of thistles.

The donkeys cannot reach the thistles, which are growing outside their paddock. "Thistles are our favorite," think all three donkeys.

Two children walk by. They stop and one asks, "What are the donkeys looking at?" The children look at the thistles.

"Yuck! It can't be those horrid prickly thistles," the other child replies.

"We'll find you some nice fresh grass," the children say to the donkeys.

The donkeys look at the children and then back to the lovely, yummy thistles and think…

 2. Talk about the story

- What are the names of the three donkeys? *(Thor, Moth and Thad are unusual names. They can be used to introduce the idea of nonsense words, which still need to be blended and read.)*
- What is a paddock?
- What do the donkeys want to eat?
- Why can't they reach the thistles?

- Why do the children say *Yuck!*?
- Why do the children walk past the donkeys' paddock? *(They are on their way to school / going to a friend's house.)*
- What do the donkeys want the children to do? *(Pick the thistles and put them in the paddock.)*
- What do the children and donkeys do next?

Story time

Further reading

Read some stories about donkeys, for example:

The Wonky Donkey song and book Craig Smith (author) and Katz Cowley (illustrator)

The Dinky Donkey song and book Craig Smith (author) and Katz Cowley (illustrator)

A House is Built for Eeyore A. A. Milne (author) and E. H. Shepard (illustrator)

Rhyme time

A haiku is a Japanese poem that has three lines with five syllables in the first line, seven in the second, and five in the last. Recite this haiku as a class or ask three children at a time to do so. You could also ask what happy thoughts the donkeys might be thinking.

Three little donkeys,
Munching prickly thistles, while
Thinking happy thoughts.

UNIT 3: Reading comprehension lesson

The three donkeys

 3. Comprehension activities

Look at Student Book page 7 with the class. Tell the children to:

1. Read the phrases and draw a picture for each one.
2. Complete the yes / no questions by circling the correct answer.
3. Read and answer the question. Encourage the children to write a complete sentence.

The children can also…
- Find all the words in the story with a <th> spelling.
- Draw a picture of the three donkeys and write their names.
- Read the passage with a partner.

 4. Plenary

Read the story again as a class, using the punctuation to read with expression and fluency. Encourage the children to pull a face and sound disgusted when they say *Yuck!*. Ask them to suggest ways to finish the last sentence.

 Further activities

- Find out more about donkeys.
- Read some stories and rhymes about donkeys.
- Find out about the horse family. (For example: *ponies, asses, zebras.*)

Learning objectives

The children are learning to:
- Listen to, discuss, and recall details from story texts.
- Link what they hear to their own experiences.
- Discuss word meanings, linking new words to those they already know.
- Use inferences and prediction.
- Recite rhymes by heart.

25

The three donkeys

UNIT 3: Writing skills lesson

1. Introductory activity

Briefly discuss what the class knows about donkeys. Ask the children what they themselves like and do not like to eat.

Remind the children to listen to others when they are speaking and to wait their turn to speak.

2. Talk about the writing

Retell the story of **The three donkeys**. Ask the children what happens at the beginning and in the middle of the story. Then ask: What happens at the end of the story? Does it end? Find out if the class remembers thatABC the three dots indicate that the last sentence is not finished. Ask some children to finish the sentence by suggesting what the donkeys are thinking. Use open-ended questions to help spark their imagination and remind them that the donkeys could be thinking anything at all. Ask the children what might happen next and to suggest how the story could end.

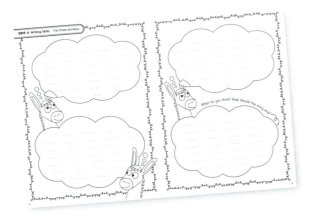

Remind the children to answer by using complete sentences.

3. Writing activity

1. Draw a big thought bubble on the board.
2. Ask some children who have not already made suggestions what the donkeys might be thinking.

As necessary, sound out any difficult words, explain any unusual spellings, and talk about any tricky words.

3. Choose one of the suggestions and model it in the thought bubble on the board.
4. Tell the children to write in thought bubbles what they think each donkey is thinking. Encourage the class to write in sentences.

The children can also…
- Write and finish the last sentence.
- Re-read their work, ensuring it makes sense.
- Write what makes them happy inside empty thought bubbles.
- Draw a picture of themselves next to their thought bubble.

4. Plenary

Share some of the children's work, either by showing it to the other children or by asking some of them to read out what they have written.

UNIT 3: Writing skills lesson

 Further activities

- Make a collage of a donkey's head.
- Look at books and comics that use thought and speech bubbles.
- Have the children draw or paint a self-portrait with their name written underneath.
- Listen to a piece of music. Talk about how the music makes the children feel. While they listen to the music, write some words, or draw a picture in a thought bubble.

 Assessment

 The child suggests something the donkeys might be thinking and can suggest or predict an ending for the story; writes some words, most of which are plausibly spelled, but uses little or no punctuation.

 The child suggests something the donkeys might be thinking and makes a plausible suggestion or prediction as to how the story might end; writes in sentences independently, using periods and with most known and regular words correctly spelled; makes plausible attempts at spelling unknown and irregular words.

 The child suggests something the donkeys might be thinking and makes a plausible suggestion or prediction as to how the story might end; writes at least one sentence independently, using some periods and plausible spellings.

Learning objectives

The children are learning to:
- Listen to, discuss, and recall details from story texts.
- Understand the concept of thought bubbles.
- Discuss what they are going to write about.
- Say a sentence.
- Write simple sentences.
- Write words using phonically plausible spellings.
- Re-read their own writing to check that it makes sense.
- Read their own writing aloud to others.

Animal alphabet

 1. Read the poem

Read the poem to the class. Ensure the children can see the text, pointing to the words as you read. Read the poem again, sounding out any difficult or unusual words, such as *kangaroos*, *quails*, or *vixens*. Check that the children know the meaning of these words. Explain that because this is a list poem it is not written in complete sentences that end in a period.

 2. Talk about the poem

Animal alphabet
Angry ants
Buzzing bees
Clapping cats
Dancing donkeys
Enormous elephants
Flying fish
Grumpy goats
Hiccuping hippos
Itching insects
Jumping jellyfish
Kicking kangaroos
Lazing lions
Mining moles
Nibbling newts
Orange octopuses
Prickly porcupines
Quiet quails
Resting robins
Squirting squid
Trampolining tigers
Upside-down umbrella birds
Vain vixens
Waddling wombats
Boxing foxes
Yelling yaks
Zigzagging zebras
...at my zoo!

Point out that...

- Each line of the poem, and the animal in it, starts with a different letter of the alphabet.
- The lines are ordered alphabetically.
- The first word of each line starts with a capital letter and the following word starts with a lower-case letter.
- The animal name words have an <s> or <es> on the end, which indicates they are plural (meaning there is more than one of them). The exception to this rule are the words *fish* and *squid*, which are irregular plurals – *fish* can mean one fish or lots of fish, while *squid* can be one squid or lots of squid.

- What are some of the animals doing? (*Which of the animals are clapping / flying / mining?*)
- Which animal is prickly?
- What **other** things could some of the animals be doing? (*Gobbling goats / hopping hippos / squirming squid*)
- Why does *boxing foxes* represent the letter <x> and not words that begin with <x>? (*A few animals do have a name beginning with <x>, but they are not well known and the <x> does not make a /ks/ sound.*)

Story time

Further reading

Read some alphabet books, for example:

A – Apple Pie Kate Greenaway

ABC Zoo Rod Campbell

P Is for Poppadoms! An Indian Alphabet Book Kabir Sehgal and Surishtha Sehgal (authors) and Hazel Ito (illustrator)

Eating the Alphabet: Fruits & Vegetables from A to Z Lois Ehlert

Rhyme time

As well as singing this rhyme to the tune of **Row, row, row your boat**, you can ask the children to recite the alphabet. Both can be done as a class, in groups, or individually.

*Squirt, squirt goes the squid,
Swimming through the sea.
Black ink spreading everywhere,
Now you can't see me!*

UNIT 4: Reading comprehension lesson

Animal alphabet

 3. Comprehension activities

Look at Student Book page 9 with the class. Tell the children to:

1. Read the phrases and draw a picture for each one.

2. Complete the yes / no questions by circling the correct answer.

3. Read and answer the question. In this instance, the children do not have to write a complete sentence.

> **The children can also...**
> - Find all the words in the poem with an <ng> spelling.
> - With a partner, think of other things some of the animals could be doing.
> - Read the poem with a partner.

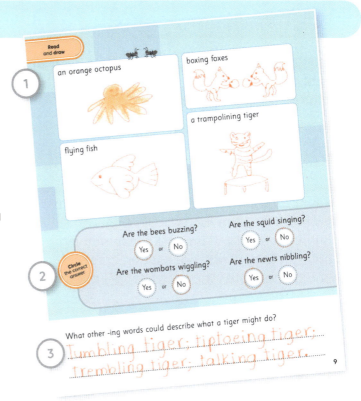

 4. Plenary

Read the poem again as a class. Encourage the children to read with expression and fluency. A different child could be chosen to read each line.

Ask some of the children to suggest some other things for the animals to do.

Further activities

- Find, and look at, books on animals from around the world.
- Read or listen to some animal stories.
- Draw, paint, or make a collage of some of the animals. These can be displayed as an alphabet or made into a class book.

Learning objectives

The children are learning to:
- Listen to, discuss, and recall details from poems.
- Discuss word meanings, linking new words to those they already know.
- Say the letters of the alphabet in order.
- Recite rhymes and poems.

UNIT 4: Writing skills lesson

Alphabet soup

1. Introductory activity

Recite the alphabet as a class. Remind the children about the **Animal alphabet** list poem. Briefly talk about how the poem is structured using the letters of the alphabet.

2. Talk about the writing

Ask the children what their favorite foods are and which letter the foods begin with. Go through the alphabet and ask for something to eat that begins with each letter, creating a food alphabet (or "alphabet soup") poem.

Encourage the children to also think of a word describing each food that begins with the same sound, creating an alliterative phrase.

Examples

- Aa: (amazing) apples
- Bb: (big) bananas
- Cc: (crunchy) coconuts
- Dd: (delightful) dates
- Ee: (excellent) eggs
- Ff: (fabulous) fish
- Gg: (good) grapes
- Hh: (healthy) honey
- Ii: (icy) ice creams
- Jj: (juicy) jams
- Kk: (kingly) kiwis
- Ll: (lovely) lemons
- Mm: (mouthwatering) mangoes
- Nn: (nourishing) noodles
- Oo: (odd-shaped) okras
- Pp: (pleasant) plums
- Qq: (quality) quinces
- Rr: (red) rice
- Ss: (spicy) stews
- Tt: (tasty) tomatoes
- Uu: (unusual) ugli fruits
- Vv: (vital) vegetables
- Ww: (wonderful) watermelons
- Xx: box of (extra) fries
- Yy: (yellow) yams
- Zz: (zesty) zucchinis

3. Writing activity

The children write their own "alphabet soup" poem. They start by writing the alphabet down the left-hand side of the page, with a new letter on each line. Then, for each letter, they think of a food or an alliterative phrase about that food and write it on the line.

If the children need extra support, they can copy the class alphabet.

The children can also...

- Re-read their work, checking the words in each line start with the correct letter.
- Go over the capital and lower-case letters with colored pens.
- Illustrate their poem with some pictures.

UNIT 4: Writing skills lesson

4. Plenary

Share some of the children's work, either by showing it to the other children or by asking some of them to read out what they have written.

Further activities

- Draw, paint, or collage food. These can be displayed as an alphabet or made into a class book.
- Complete some alphabet jigsaws.
- Make up some other alphabet list poems with birds, names, or dinosaurs, for example.

Assessment

The child suggests a food for each letter of the alphabet, and writes the word using phonically plausible spelling.

The child suggests and writes an alliterative phrase for each letter of the alphabet; writes independently, using correct spellings for most known and regular words; makes plausible attempts at spelling unknown and irregular words.

The child suggests a food for each letter of the alphabet and writes the word independently, using plausible spelling; thinks of, and writes, an alliterative phrase for some of the foods.

Learning objectives

The children are learning to:
- Discuss what they are going to write about.
- Say the alphabet and use it to structure a poem.
- Identify words beginning with certain letters.
- Understand and identify alliteration.
- Understand that poems do not have to rhyme.
- Write words using phonically plausible spellings.
- Re-read their writing to check that it makes sense.

UNIT 5: Reading comprehension lesson

An Australian animal park

 1. Read the postcard

Read the postcard to the class, starting with the name and address. Ensure the children can see the text, pointing to words as you read. Read the postcard again, sounding out any difficult or unusual words, such as *Australian*, *quokkas*, *tongues*, *platypuses*, and *koala*. Check that the children know the meaning of these words. Point out the capital letters in the proper nouns (including *Granny* and *Grandpa*) and in the adjective *Australian*, which has a capital letter because the word comes from the proper noun *Australia*.

 2. Talk about the postcard

Look at how the postcard is written. It starts with *Dear...*, giving the name of the person or people the postcard is for, and finishes with the signature of the person writing the card.

Explain that...

...the story **A visit to the aquarium** (Unit 1) was written about the children Josh and Sasha; the story was not written by them. This postcard is written by Zack himself, so he uses the pronouns *I* and *we*. That is called writing in the first person.

- Talk about first names and surnames. *(Check that the children know and can spell their own surnames.)*
- Where did Zack go?
- What animals did he see?
- Why did he like the quokkas best?
- What happened at the "Meet the Animals" talk?
- Why do you think no one else wantedto touch the millipede?
- Who could *we* be? (For example: *family, parents, siblings, friends.*)
- Has anyone in the class ever been to a wildlife park?

Story time

Further reading

Read some stories about postcards, for example:

The Jolly Postman Janet and Allan Ahlberg

Dragon Post Emma Yarlett

Paddington's Post Michael Bond (author) and R. W. Alley (illustrator)

Rhyme time

Encourage the children to repeat this song with you – to the tune of **Row, row, row your boat**:

*Quack, quack go the ducks,
Squabbling on the pond.
Squirm, splash, squiggle and quack,
All that corn is mine!*

UNIT 5: Reading comprehension lesson

An Australian animal park

3. Comprehension activities

Look at Student Book page 11 with the class. Tell the children to:

1. Read the phrases and draw a picture for each one.
2. Complete the yes / no questions by circling the correct answer.
3. Read and answer the question. Encourage the children to write a complete sentence.

> **The children can also...**
> - Find all the words in the postcard with a <qu> spelling.
> - Read the postcard with a partner.
> - Underline all the proper nouns with a black pencil.

4. Plenary

Read the postcard again as a class. Encourage the children to read with expression and fluency.

Further activities

- Talk about different types of homes such as animal homes (*a lion's den, dog's kennel, horse's stable*) or famous addresses (*Buckingham Palace, Sydney Opera House, The White House,* for example).
- Look at maps and atlases.
- Find out where Australia is and what animals live there.

Learning objectives

The children are learning to:
- Listen to, discuss, and recall details from different types of text.
- Link what they hear or read to their own experiences.
- Understand some grammatical terminology (first person).
- Discuss word meanings, linking new words to those they already know.
- Recite rhymes, poems, and songs.

UNIT 5: Writing skills lesson

Addresses and postcards

 1. Introductory activity

Briefly discuss the postcard from Zack and talk about what an address is for: it tells us exactly where someone or something is in the world. Look at some more postcards, as well as books like *The Jolly Postman* by Janet and Allan Ahlberg.

 2. Talk about the writing

Discuss the reasons why people send postcards and ask the children why it is important to write the address correctly.

>
> **Point out that...**
>
> ...some of the writing in a postcard is formal because it has to be written in a certain way. (*Name and address on right-hand side; message on left-hand side, starting* Dear...).

Find out if any children know their own address, then think up some imaginary ones, such as:

> Inky Mouse
> The Mouse Hole
> Zack's House
>
> Bee
> The Bee Hive
> East Orchard
> Moat Farm

If the children do not know their own address, you can use the school address.

 3. Writing activity

1. Show the children how to make a postcard. Turn a sheet of paper so the widest part is at the top and bottom, then draw a line down the middle to separate the address from the message.

2. Ask the children to write a postcard to someone they know, telling them about somewhere they have been. If the children do not know the address, they can use the school's address instead.

3. When the children have finished writing their postcard, they can turn it over and draw a picture on the front.

> **The children can also...**
> - Re-read their work, ensuring it makes sense.
> - Make up names and addresses for storybook characters and write them on envelopes.
> - Share their work with a partner.

34

UNIT 5: Writing skills lesson

4. Plenary

Share some of the children's work, either by showing it to the other children or by asking some of them to read out what they have written.

Further activities

- Try writing their signature as many times as possible, using different colors and pens on a sheet of paper.
- Design some stamps.
- Collect some postcards together and find out where in the world they have come from.

Assessment

The child writes some words or sentences using phonically plausible spelling; attempts to write an address or part of it.

The child writes a message starting *Dear...* and signs it; writes independently, using some periods and plausible spellings; knows how an address is written and attempts to write it correctly.

The child writes a message starting *Dear...* and signs it; writes independently, using correct spellings for most known and regular words; makes plausible attempts at spelling irregular and unknown words; knows how an address is written and can write it correctly.

Learning objectives

The children are learning to:
- Discuss what they are going to write about.
- Say their surname and address.
- Understand what a signature is.
- Write their full name and address.
- Write in the style of a postcard or letter.
- Write words using phonically plausible spellings.
- Re-read their writing to check that it makes sense.

UNIT 6: Reading comprehension lesson

Go, go, go-kart racing!

 1. Read the story

Read the story **Go, go, go-kart racing!** to the class. Ensure the children can see the text, pointing to the words as you read. Read the story again, sounding out any difficult or unusual words, such as *go-kart, suggested, catch, slug,* and *whizzed.* Check that the children know the meaning of these words. Point out the capital letters and punctuation, such as periods, speech marks, and exclamation points.

 2. Talk about the story

- What is a go-kart race or soap box derby?
- Have the children ever been in a go-kart?
- Why did Snake say Bee's go-kart moves like a slug?
  (Snake said Bee's go-kart is slow to annoy her.)
- Why is the word *"Byeeeeee!"* written with the extra <e> letters? *(To show that Bee was going quickly past Snake.)*
- Why did Inky shout *"Wait for me!"*?
- What happened to Bee?
- Why do you think Bee crashed?
- Why wasn't it a fair race?
  (They did not all start at the same time.)

Go, go, go-kart racing!

Inky, Bee, and Snake had made go-karts for the Soap Box Derby race.

"Let's try them out on the farm track," suggested Bee.

At the start of the track, Bee waved and cried, "Byeeeeee!" as she shot off down the hill.

"I'll catch you up, Bee. Your go-kart moves like a slug!" yelled Snake.

"Wait for me!" shouted Inky, putting on her scarf and helmet.

Bee whizzed through the farmyard and looked back to see where the others were. She missed the bend and…

…CRASH!

Snake and Inky rushed to help Bee. Her go-kart was on its side.

"Ouch!" Bee cried. "I was whizzing along and suddenly the go-kart flipped over. I hit the ground hard, but I'm all right."

12

Point out that…

…the word CRASH is in capital letters.

Explain that this shows it is an important word in the story and that the crash made a loud noise. Look at the shape the word is written in. Why might that shape have been used?

Story time

Further reading

Read some stories about go-kart racing, for example:

Mrs Armitage on Wheels Quentin Blake

The Great Go-Kart Race Jonathan Litton (author) and Magalí Mansilla (illustrator)

Turbo Bunnies Matty Long

Rhyme time

Encourage the children to repeat this rhyme with you – to the tune of **Row, row, row your boat**:

> *Vroom, vroom go the cars,*
> *Racing round the track,*
> *Far and fast around the track,*
> *And then they all come back.*

UNIT 6: Reading comprehension lesson

3. Comprehension activities

Look at Student Book page 13 with the class. Tell the children to:

1. Read the phrases and draw a picture for each one.
2. Complete the yes / no questions by circling the correct answer.
3. Read and answer the question. Encourage the children to write a complete sentence.
4. Find three common noun words in the story and write them on the lines.

> **The children can also...**
> - Find all the words in the story with an <ar> spelling.
> - Read the story with a partner.
> - Write a sentence from the story and draw a picture to illustrate their words.

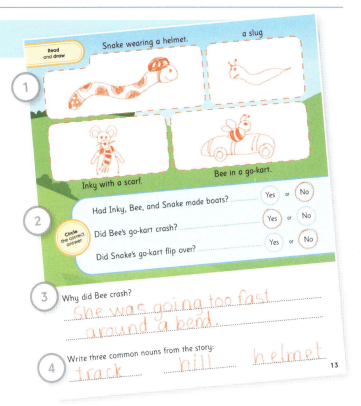

4. Plenary

Read the story again as a class. Encourage the children to read with expression and fluency, especially when they say the words *Byeeeeee!* and *CRASH!*.

Further activities

- Find and look at pictures of go-karts.
- Watch a video about a soap box derby.
- Make model go-karts out of plastic bricks and race them on a track.
- Look at, and discuss, what else has wheels.

Learning objectives

The children are learning to:
- Listen to, discuss, and recall details from stories.
- Link what they read or hear to their own experiences.
- Discuss word meanings, linking new words to those they already know.
- Use inference and prediction.
- Recite rhymes by heart.

UNIT 6: Writing skills lesson

The go-kart race

1. Introductory activity

Briefly discuss the story **Go, go, go-kart racing!**. Talk about what happens at the beginning of the story (the start of the race), then in the middle of the story (the race itself), and at the end (when Bee crashes).

2. Talk about the writing

Ask the children what they think it would feel like to go racing. Use visual prompts, such as pictures of go-karts and go-kart races, maps of tracks and, if possible, watch a video of a soap box derby.

Identify the different parts of a go-kart (wheels, seat, steering, brakes), and discuss what themes the children would choose for their kart.

Show the class a simple map of a race track or use a play mat with a roadway or race track design.

Ask some children to take turns "driving" a toy car around the track, telling the other children what is happening as they do so.

Alternatively, the children could create their own track on a length of rolled-out wallpaper, drawing or adding pictures of walls, trees, ponds, puddles, and beehives, for example. Then, instead of using a toy car, the children could walk around the track themselves, describing in words what is happening in their imagination. (For example: *"I am first across the starting line and whizz down the track toward the first bend. I go through a puddle. The water splashes up and I cannot see."*)

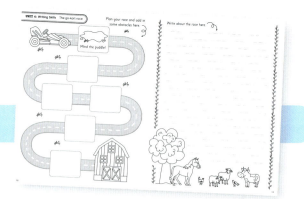

3. Writing activity

Tell the children to either retell the **Go, go, go-kart racing!** story or write their own story about a race. Use the class map or track to start the story. Who is racing? What happens at the start? What goes on during the race? What happens at the end?

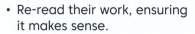

The children can also...

- Re-read their work, ensuring it makes sense.
- Draw a picture of the race or race track.
- Share their work with a partner.

4. Plenary

Share some of the children's work, either by showing it to the other children or by asking some of them to read out what they have written.

UNIT 6: Writing skills lesson

 Further activities

- Design and draw a picture of a go-kart, labeling the different parts.
- Plan how to customize a go-kart, adding fun or useful things, such as a drink dispenser, umbrella, or even a dog seat.
- Write SMASH or CRASH in capital letters and put colored zigzag lines around the words. Think of other words that could replace *smash* or *crash*, such as *bang*, *thump*, *wallop*, *thud*, and *crunch*.

 Assessment

The child writes some words or sentences that are plausibly spelled but uses little or no punctuation; can talk about what happens at the beginning, middle, and end of the story.

The child retells the story in sentences, using ideas from the story and adding further details from the class-made track; writes at least one page independently, using periods and correct spellings for most known and regular words; makes plausible attempts at spelling unknown and irregular words; ideas are ordered and the story has a clear beginning, middle, and end.

The child retells the basic story, writing at least half a page independently, and uses some periods, capital letters and plausible spellings; can imagine racing along the track and talks about doing so; uses some of the ideas inspired by the class-made track in their writing, which shows a beginning, middle, and end.

Learning objectives

The children are learning to:
- Discuss what they are going to write about.
- Understand narrative (that a story has a beginning, middle, and end).
- Retell a story using visual prompts.
- Use a simple plan (story map) to support or organize their writing.
- Write simple sentences to retell a story.
- Write words using phonically plausible spellings.
- Re-read their writing to check that it makes sense.

UNIT 7: Reading comprehension lesson

My week

 1. Read the diary

Read the diary to the class. Ensure the children can see the text, pointing to the words as you read. Read the diary again, sounding out any difficult or unusual words, such as *Grandma*, *banana*, and *squirrels*. Check that the children know the meaning of these words. Explain that when people write in diaries, they are usually writing about themselves. When they do this, they write in the first person, using the pronouns *I* and *we*.

 2. Talk about the diary

- What is a diary?
- Where did the person writing the diary go on Monday?
- What did they make with Grandma?
- What might Grandma's dog be called?
- Why didn't the squirrels get any corn?
- When was the farm trip?
- Where was Zack's party?
- What day did the person writing the diary like best and why?

Explain that...

...a diary is written by someone about the things they have been doing. This means that the writing is about what has been done in the past, so it will say, *"We went to an aquarium"* not *"We go..."* and *"We saw lots of..."* not *"We see...".*

Story time

Further reading

Read some stories and books about days of the week, for example:

Days of the Week
Anna Milbourne (author)
and Grace Habib (illustrator)

The Very Hungry Caterpillar
Eric Carle

Rhyme time

Encourage the children
to repeat this rhyme with you:

"
Monday's child is fair of face,
Tuesday's child is full of grace.
Wednesday's child is full of woe,
Thursday's child has far to go.
Friday's child is loving and giving,
Saturday's child works hard for a living.
But the child that is born on the Sabbath day,
Is bonny and blithe, good and gay.
"

UNIT 7: Reading comprehension lesson

3. Comprehension activities

Look at Student Book page 15 with the class. Tell the children to:

1. Read the phrases and draw a picture for each one.
2. Complete the yes / no questions by circling the correct answer.
3. Read and answer the questions. Encourage the children to write in complete sentences.

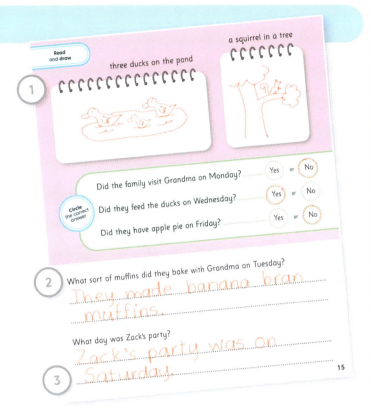

The children can also...
- Write the days of the week in order, remembering to give each day a capital letter.
- With a partner, say the days of the week in order from memory.

4. Plenary

Read the diary again as a class. Encourage the children to use the punctuation to help them read with expression and fluency. Different children could be chosen to read each day's diary entry.

Further activities

- Look at some diaries.
- Talk about a hobby (like swimming or baking) to the rest of the class.
- Think about some of the things that people might record in their diary and make a list. (For example: *books they read, activities they did, meals they ate.*)

Learning objectives

The children are learning to:
- Listen to, discuss, and recall details from different types of texts.
- Link what they hear or read to their own experiences.
- Talk about the features of a diary
- Recite rhymes by heart.

UNIT 7: Writing skills lesson

Days of the week

 1. Introductory activity

Ask the class to recite the days of the week, and explain that people use diaries to record what happened on certain days. Show the children some diaries. As well as keeping a diary about what they did each day, people also keep diaries to record other things, such as the weather, appointments, or things they are going to do in the future.

 2. Talk about the writing

Ask some of the class to complete the sentence, "*Last Monday, I…*". Then ask the children to think about what they did last week. Choose a few children to tell the group what they did. (*Last Wednesday, I had my swimming class. On Friday, I went to after-school club.*)

 3. Writing activity

1. Write *Monday* on the board. Remind the class that since *Monday* is a proper noun the word needs a capital letter. Point out that the <o> is making an /u/ sound.

2. Ask some children to say a sentence about what they did on a Monday. Choose one of the sentences to model to the class. Explain you are not going to write *Monday* because the day is already written on the board. Model the rest of the sentence, writing it underneath the word *Monday*.

If the children need extra support, provide pictures of objects or activities, such as a football, dance shoes, or a recorder.

3. Tell the children to fill in their diary for the week. First, they write the day of the week. Then, on a separate line, they write about something they did on that day. The children write an entry for every day of the week.

Remind the children that sentences start with a capital letter and end with a period, and remind them to leave spaces between words. Sound out any difficult words and talk about any tricky words.

The children can also…

- Draw some pictures to illustrate their diary.
- Re-read their work, ensuring it makes sense.
- Create a poem inspired by Eric Carle's **The Very Hungry Caterpillar**, such as The Very Hungry Snake:

   *On Monday I had chocolate cake,
   On Tuesday I had two cheeseburgers,
   On Wednesday I had fish fingers and beans,
   On Thursday I had four apple pies,
   On Friday I had curry, samosas and naan,
   On Saturday I had six pepperoni pizzas,
   On Sunday I had chicken, rice, peas, and hummingbird cake. Yummy!
   …and on Sunday night I had a stomach ache!*

- Find out what is in a hummingbird cake.

42

UNIT 7: Writing skills lesson

4. Plenary

Share some of the children's work, either by showing it to the other children or by asking some of them to read out what they have written.

Further activities

- Keep a class diary for a week, recording what the children do each day.
- Copy, trace, or write inside different fonts and styles for the days of the week.
- Write out the days of the week, then cut up the list. Have the children work together to put them back in the correct order.

Assessment

The child writes a word or phrase for each day, using plausible spellings but with little or no punctuation; can read the days of the week; can say the days of the week in order with some help.

The child writes a couple of sentences for each day independently, using periods and correct spellings for most known and regular words; makes plausible attempts at spelling unknown and irregular words; knows what they usually do each day; can read and correctly spell the days of the week; can say the days of the week in order.

The child writes at least a sentence for each day independently, using some periods and plausible spellings; can read the days of the week and spell most of them correctly; can say the days of the week in order.

Learning objectives

The children are learning to:
- Discuss what they are going to write about and use a simple plan to support or organize their writing.
- Understand different types of writing (a diary).
- Understand some grammatical terminology (first person).
- Write simple sentences to create a sequence of events (narrative).
- Read their own writing aloud to others.

Puffins

1. Read the text

Read the text to the class. Ensure the children can see the words, pointing to them as you read. Read the text again, sounding out any difficult or unusual words, such as *colorful*, *markings*, *burrows*, *puffling*, *bills*, *August*, and *adults*. Check that the children know the meaning of these words.

Point out the scientific name (*Fratercula arctica*) and the pronunciation guide that appears underneath between two forward slashes (/.../). Explain that all animals have a scientific name and, because these are Latin words, the names can be difficult to read. Say the sounds and blend the words with the children: /f-r-a-t-er-k-ue-l-a ar-k-t-i-k-a/.

2. Talk about the text

Explain that if someone wants to find out more about puffins, they can look in a book or find information on the internet. Explain that books about real things are called *nonfiction* books, and those with stories or poems are called *fiction* books.

- What sort of animals are puffins?
- What colors are they?
- What is a young puffin called?
- What is a *wingspan*? (*The distance between the ends of each wing when they are stretched out.*)
- Where do puffins nest?
- Why might puffins be called *sea parrots*? (*Because they have colorful beaks like those of parrots.*)
- Where do puffins spend the winter months?

Story time

Further reading

Read some stories and books about puffins and other seabirds, for example:

Puffins (National Geographic Pre-Reader) Maya Myers

Puffin (Nature Storybooks) Martin Jenkins (author) and Jenni Desmond (illustrator)

Puffin Peter Petr Horáček

Rhyme time

Encourage the children to repeat this rhyme with you:

*Little Miss Muffet,
Sat on a tuffet,
Eating her curds and whey.
A great big spider,
Sat down beside her,
And frightened Miss Muffet away.*

UNIT 8: Reading comprehension lesson

3. Comprehension activities

Look at Student Book page 17 with the class. Tell the children to:

1. Read the phrase and draw a picture.
2. Complete the yes / no questions by circling the correct answer.
3. Read and answer the questions. Encourage the children to write in complete sentences.

The children can also...
- Find all the words in the text with an <ff> spelling.
- Read the passage with a partner.
- Write about puffins and draw a picture of a puffling.

4. Plenary

Read the text again as a class. Encourage the children to use the punctuation to help them read with expression and fluency.

Further activities

- Draw or paint real or imaginary birds.
- Look at some books about birds.
- Visit a library to find nonfiction and fiction books about birds.

Learning objectives

The children are learning to:
- Listen to, discuss, and recall details from nonfiction.
- Discuss word meanings, linking new words to those they already know.
- Select different texts for a specific purpose.
- Use images to support their understanding of the text.
- Recite rhymes by heart.

45

UNIT 8: Writing skills lesson

Writing nonfiction

Before class
Find some nonfiction books about different birds or print out some information about specific birds from the internet. This could be done as a class visit to the school library.

1. Introductory activity

Remind the children about the terms *fiction* and *nonfiction*. Discuss whether the class thinks the writing about puffins is fiction or nonfiction. Ask the children what they remember about puffins.

2. Talk about the writing

Show the children some books or information about different kinds of birds. Choose birds that are familiar to the children. Look at how the information is presented and what it tells readers about the birds.

3. Writing activity

1. Tell the children that they are going to pick one of the birds to find out more about, for a piece of writing. (This can be done individually or in groups.) The children need to find out, for example, what the bird looks like, where it lives and nests, what it eats, and so on.
2. The children write about the bird using the facts they have discovered. They should be encouraged to write independently and to try spelling words, even if they are unsure of the correct spelling.
3. The children can also draw a picture of the bird or print one out from the internet and add it to their writing.

4. Plenary

Share some of the children's work, either by showing it to the other children or by asking some of them to read out what they have written.

UNIT 8: Writing skills lesson

Further activities

- Annotate a picture or photograph of a bird. Labels can include *wing*, *leg*, *foot*, *beak* or *bill*, *eye*, *tail*, *feather/s*.
- Use the annotated pictures and the children's writing to make a class book or display.
- If possible, hang some simple bird feeders outside the classroom.
- Have a birdwatch and identify the birds you see. Find out about some of them.

Assessment

The child reads the name of the bird; writes (copies) the name correctly and draws a picture; finds out something about the bird; uses plausible spellings for most words but with little or no punctuation; understands that the text is about a real creature.

The child reads and extracts information from the text; writes some sentences about the bird based on this information independently and writes a few sentences to accompany their picture; uses periods and correct spellings for most known and regular words; makes plausible attempts at spelling irregular and unknown words; knows and understands the difference between real and imaginary; knows and understands the terms *fiction* and *nonfiction*.

The child reads and extracts some information from the text; writes some sentences about the bird; writes independently, using some periods and plausible spellings; knows and understands the difference between real and imaginary; may use the terms *fiction* and *nonfiction*.

Learning objectives

The children are learning to:
- Discuss what they are going to write about.
- Understand different types of writing (fiction and nonfiction).
- Extract information from something they have read.
- Write simple sentences in a sequence to order information.
- Re-read their writing to check it makes sense.

47

UNIT 9: Reading comprehension lesson

Hickory dickory dock

 1. Read the rhyme

Read the rhyme to the class. Ensure the children can see the text, pointing out the words as you read. Read the rhyme again, sounding out any difficult or unusual words or terms, such as *to and fro*. Check that the children know the meaning of these words and terms.

> **Explain that...**
> - The words *hickory dickory* are nonsense words, so they have no meaning.
> - These words rhyme, because the sounds match after the first letter.

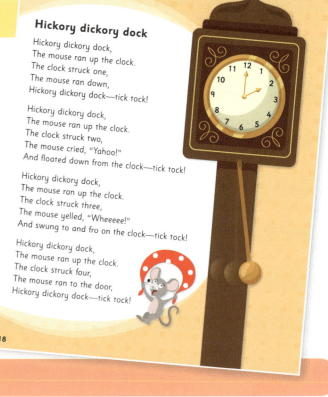

Hickory dickory dock

Hickory dickory dock,
The mouse ran up the clock.
The clock struck one,
The mouse ran down,
Hickory dickory dock—tick tock!

Hickory dickory dock,
The mouse ran up the clock.
The clock struck two,
The mouse cried, "Yahoo!"
And floated down from the clock—tick tock!

Hickory dickory dock,
The mouse ran up the clock.
The clock struck three,
The mouse yelled, "Wheeeee!"
And swung to and fro on the clock—tick tock!

Hickory dickory dock,
The mouse ran up the clock.
The clock struck four,
The mouse ran to the door,
Hickory dickory dock—tick tock!

18

 2. Talk about the rhyme

Point out how a rhyme is arranged in groups of lines called *verses*. The lines in each verse have a particular rhythm and some of the words rhyme with each other.

- What does *struck* mean?
- Why did the clock strike?
- What is special about the words: *two* and *Yahoo!*; *three* and *Wheeeee!*; *four* and *door*?
- Why does the rhyme say the mouse *floated down*?
- What did the mouse use to float?
- Does anyone in the class know or remember other rhymes?

> **Point out that...**
>
> ...a grandfather clock is a tall clock with a long pendulum that swings from side to side as it keeps time. The part of the clock that controls the pendulum makes the noise *tick tock*. When the mouse is swinging *to and fro*, it is swinging on the pendulum.

Story time

Further reading

Read some books with rhymes, for example:

The Cat in the Hat Dr. Seuss

You Can't Take an Elephant on the Bus Patricia Cleveland-Peck (author) and David Tazzyman (illustrator)

Hairy Maclary Lynley Dodd

Rhyme time

Encourage the children to repeat this rhyme with you:

> One, two, buckle my shoe.
> Three, four, knock on the door.
> Five, six, pick up sticks.
> Seven, eight, lay them straight.
> Nine, ten, a good fat hen.

48

UNIT 9: Reading comprehension lesson

Hickory dickory dock

3. Comprehension activities

Look at Student Book page 19 with the class. Tell the children to:

1. Write the numbers 1 – 12 in the circles around the clock face. Draw the hands on the clock to show one o'clock.
2. Complete the yes / no questions by circling the correct answer.
3. Read and answer the questions. Encourage the children to write in complete sentences.
4. Find the words in the verses that rhyme with the number words. Then find the words that start with the letters <cl>, <st> and <cr>.

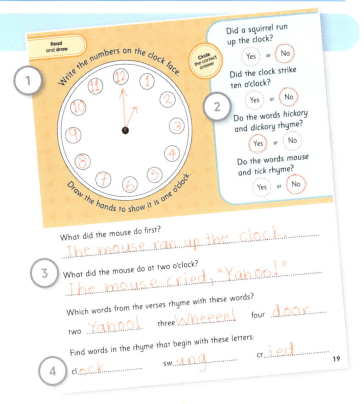

> **The children can also...**
> - Find all the words in the rhyme with a <ck> spelling.
> - Read and remember the rhyme and say it with, or to, a partner.

4. Plenary

Read the rhyme again as a class. Encourage the children to read with fluency and expression, especially when they reach words such as *Yahoo!* and *Wheeeee!*.

Further activities

- Draw a picture of Inky mouse.
- Illustrate some other nursery rhymes for a display or class book.
- Practice telling the time.
- Find out about different types of clock.

Learning objectives

The children are learning to:
- Listen to, discuss, and recall details from rhymes.
- Appreciate rhymes and poems, and recite some by heart.
- Discuss word meanings, linking new words to those they already know.

49

UNIT 9: Writing skills lesson

Rhyming words

 1. Introductory activity

Recite the rhyme **Hickory dickory dock** as a class.

 2. Talk about rhymes

Explain that words that rhyme end in the same sounds. Stress that it is the sound that is important not the spelling. Rhyming involves playing with words and sounds, and sometimes the words or sentences in a rhyme can be somewhat silly.

Write these sentences on the board and read them out to the class:

I am Snake.
I love to eat cake.

Look at and identify the rhyming words. Point out that the rhyming words are at the end of sentences. Do the same for the sentences:

I am Inky Mouse.
I live in a house.

I am Bee.
I like drinking tea.

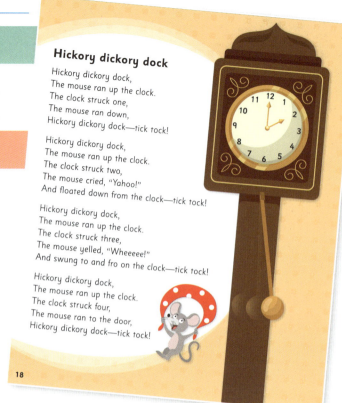

Hickory dickory dock

Hickory dickory dock,
The mouse ran up the clock.
The clock struck one,
The mouse ran down,
Hickory dickory dock—tick tock!

Hickory dickory dock,
The mouse ran up the clock.
The clock struck two,
The mouse cried, "Yahoo!"
And floated down from the clock—tick tock!

Hickory dickory dock,
The mouse ran up the clock.
The clock struck three,
The mouse yelled, "Wheeeee!"
And swung to and fro on the clock—tick tock!

Hickory dickory dock,
The mouse ran up the clock.
The clock struck four,
The mouse ran to the door,
Hickory dickory dock—tick tock!

18

 3. Writing activity

1. Ask the children to copy the three pairs of sentences and draw a picture to illustrate each pair.

2. Then look at some rhyming words with the class. (For example: *hare, air, hair; lizard, blizzard; gecko, echo; bug, slug, hug; cow, now; crocodile, smile; bat, cat, splat; giraffe, graph, laugh; parrot, carrot; fish, dish; seal, wheel, meal; aardvark, dark.*) The children choose an animal name and a word that rhymes with the animal. First they make up a short phrase ending with the animal (for example: *The hopping hare*) and then complete the sentence, making sure they finish with the other rhyming word (for example: *The hopping hare jumps high in the air.*).

Other examples:
A green and scaly crocodile gave me a great big toothy smile.
The armored aardvark was afraid of the dark.

3. Ask the children to draw a picture to illustrate their rhyme. (These can be made into a display or class book.)

The children can also...

- Choose more pairs of words and make sentences that rhyme.

- Use the Consonant Blends Wheel, if available, to help find words that rhyme. (For example: *flip, clip, blip, trip, drip, skip, snip.*)

UNIT 9: Writing skills lesson

 4. Plenary

Share some of the children's work, either by showing it to the other children or by asking some children to read out one of their rhyming sentences.

 Further activities

Learn some other nursery rhymes. (For example: **Row, row, row your boat**, **Humpty Dumpty**, **Twinkle, twinkle, little star** and **Hey diddle diddle**.)

 Assessment

The child can hear the rhymes and match the rhyming words and sentences with some help or prompting; attempts to think of two sentences with the rhyming words at the end; writes some words and sentences using phonically plausible spelling.

The child can hear the rhymes and match the rhyming words and sentences; thinks of two sentences with the rhyming words at the end; writes the sentences independently, using correct spelling for most known and regular words; makes plausible attempts at spelling irregular and unknown words.

The child can hear the rhymes and match the rhyming words and sentences, possibly with some help or prompting; thinks of two sentences with rhyming words at the end; writes the sentences independently, using phonically plausible spellings.

Learning objectives

The children are learning to:
- Discuss what they are going to write about.
- Understand different types of writing (rhyming words and couplets).
- Think of a sentence ending with a specific word.
- Write simple sentences in a sequence.
- Write words using phonically plausible spellings.
- Recite rhymes and poems.

UNIT 10: Reading comprehension lesson

The Wind and the Sun: a play

 ## 1. Read the play

Read the play to the class. Ensure the children can see the words, pointing to them as you read. Read the play again, sounding out any difficult or unusual words, such as *argument, wearing,* and *huddles.* Check that the children know the meaning of these words.

The Wind and the Sun

Narrator:	The Wind…
Wind:	(Puffs and blows loudly.)
Narrator:	…and the Sun…
Sun:	(Smiles, showing open hands either side of face.)
Narrator:	…were having an argument.
Wind:	I am so strong!
Narrator:	…shouted the Wind, making the windmill's sails spin around.
Sun:	(Smiling and shaking head.) No, I don't think so.
Narrator:	Just then, the Wind saw someone wearing a big coat walking uphill.
Person:	(Walks slowly across stage, then stops and looks around.)
Wind:	I will show you I am stronger!
Narrator:	…boasted the Wind.
Wind:	(Starts blowing and blowing.) I will blow that coat away!
Narrator:	The Wind blew and blew but…
Person:	(Person shivers and huddles under the coat, holding the collar tightly.) Brrrrr!
Narrator:	…the coat did not blow away.
Sun:	(Smiling, showing open hands either side of face.) My turn…
Narrator:	…smiled the Sun. It got hotter…
Person:	(Wipes brow with hand.) It's getting hot.
Narrator:	…and hotter. It was much too hot to wear such a big coat.
Person:	(Takes off coat and walks off.) I'm too hot.
Narrator:	The Wind stormed off…
Wind:	(Waves arms, blowing and huffing, and stomps off, looking grumpy.)
Narrator:	…and the Sun continued to smile and shine.
Sun:	(Smiles.)

 ## 2. Talk about the play

Discuss with the class what a play is: acting out a story on a stage instead of reading a story in a book.

Look at how the play is set out on the page, with the name of the character who is speaking the words on the left followed by the actual words spoken by that person on the right. Point out that there are no speech marks and that instructions for the actors are in brackets and often not in full sentences.

- What did the Wind say he could do?
- Did the Wind succeed? Why not?
- What did the Sun do?
- Why did the person take off their coat?
- Why was the Wind angry and the Sun happy?
- What is the moral of this fable? (*Size and strength do not always win a competition; sometimes gentle persuasion gets better results.*)

Explain that…

- Fables are stories that have a moral, which is a message that teaches people about how to behave in the world.
- This fable was written by a man called Aesop. He lived a long time ago in ancient Greece and told stories to teach and entertain people. Stories and fables can help us to learn more about life, especially about people and things that are different to ourselves and our own experiences.

Story time

Further reading

Read some other books that retell this fable, for example:

The Contest between the Sun and the Wind: An Aesop's Fable retold by Heather Forest and Susan Gaber (illustrator)

The North Wind and the Sun (Aesop in Rhyme) Sigal Adler (author) and Abira Das (illustrator)

The North Wind & the Sun: A Lesson in Respect Grace Hansen

Rhyme time

Encourage the children to repeat this rhyme with you:

> *When the North Wind does blow,*
> *We shall have snow,*
> *And what will poor robin do then, poor thing?*
> *He'll sit in a barn,*
> *And keep himself warm,*
> *And hide his head under his wing, poor thing.*

An alternative is the poem **Granny** by Spike Milligan, which gives a comical account of the effects of a windy day on Granny.

UNIT 10: Reading comprehension lesson

3. Comprehension activities

Look at Student Book page 21 with the class. Tell the children to:

1. Read the sentences and draw the two pictures.
2. Complete the yes / no questions by circling the correct answer.
3. Read and answer the questions. Encourage the children to write in complete sentences.

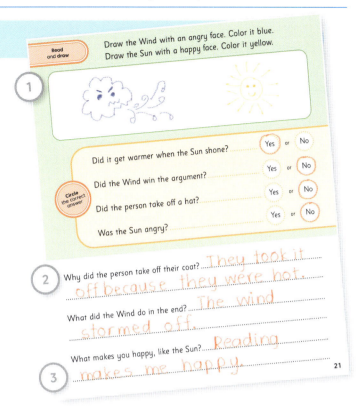

> **The children can also...**
> - Read the play with a partner or group.
> - Draw a picture of the Sun and Wind arguing, and write what they say in speech bubbles.

4. Plenary

Read the play again as a class. Some of the children could be chosen to read the different parts.

Further activities

- Find out about different types of weather.
- Talk about emotions and what makes you happy or angry.
- Look at some emojis together, then draw faces or emojis that show different emotions.

Learning objectives

The children are learning to:
- Listen to, discuss, and recall details from different types of writing.
- Become familiar with, and retell, traditional stories and rhymes.
- Discuss word meanings, linking new words to those they already know.
- Use prediction.

The Wind and the Sun: a play

Before class

Ensure all the children have access to a copy of the play, which is in the Student Book on page 20.

This lesson does not include any writing, but gives the children the opportunity to act out the play. This will also prepare them for rewriting the fable in next week's Writing skills class for unit 11.

1. Introductory activity

Remind the class about the play **The Wind and the Sun**. Briefly discuss the play and talk about its different characters. Ask the children what happened at the beginning, middle, and end of the play. Can the children remember the moral of the story?

2. Read the play

Read the play to the class. Remind the children that the names of the characters who are speaking always appear on the left-hand side. Explain that when the children are reading the play, they can say these names. If the children are acting the play, however, they do not read the names.

Point out that...

...in this play, the words and actions for each character are in a different color (black for the narrator, blue for the Wind, orange for the Sun, and green for the person.)

Choose some children to be the narrator, the Wind, the Sun, and the person. (The teacher can be the narrator if necessary.) Read through the play, with the selected children saying the lines.

3. Act out the play

1. Read through the play again but this time ask the children to act out the play. (For example: *the narrator can stand on one side while the Wind and the Sun stand facing each other. The person walks slowly across the "stage" and so on.*)
2. Divide the children into groups of four.
3. Give them copies of the play or have it on the board so it can be seen by everyone.
4. The groups of children act out the play.

The children can also...

- Draw a picture of, and write about, part of the play.
- Choose some groups to perform the play for the whole class.

UNIT 10: Writing skills lesson

54

UNIT 10: Writing skills lesson

 4. Plenary

Discuss whether the children enjoyed acting the play. Who did they think was good at being the Wind or the Sun and why? Could they improve their performance? What props might they need?

 Further activities

- Look at other fables by other authors.
- Choose another fable to act out together.
- Find other plays to read.
- Find out more about the wind and the sun.

 Assessment

The child understands that they are pretending to be a character; can say or remember the words for the character with some prompting.

The child understands that they are pretending to be a character; can read or remember the words for their character; puts a lot of expression into the words.

The child understands that they are pretending to be a character; can read or remember the words for the character; puts some expression into the words.

Learning objectives

The children are learning to:
- Listen to, discuss, and recall details from a play.
- Understand different types of writing (play and fable).
- Discuss what they are going to act out.

UNIT 11: Reading comprehension lesson

The Wind and the Sun

 1. Read the fable

Read the story to the class. Ensure the children can see the text, pointing to the words as you read. Read the story again, sounding out any difficult or unusual words, such as *sway, glinted,* and *shrugged*. Check that the children know the meaning of these words.

> **Point out that...**
> ...the speech marks are there to indicate the words a character speaks.

 2. Talk about the fable

- Why did the Wind think he was so strong?
- Why do you think he blew clouds across the Sun's face?
- Why is the word *rubbish* written as *rrrubbbishhhh!*
- Why does the story use words like *howled* and *glinted* instead of *said*?
- How do you think the wind was feeling?
- Can you remember what the moral of the story is?
- How is this text different from last week's? (*In unit 10, the story is presented as the script for a play, with the name of the character speaking on the left, followed by the words being spoken on the right. No speech marks are used.*)

The Wind and the Sun

The Wind liked to think he was very strong. He enjoyed seeing the trees and grass sway when he was tearing about.

One day, he met the Sun. "Wow!" he cried as he puffed clouds across the Sun's face. "I am stronger than you!" he howled.

"I don't think you are," glinted the Sun, smiling.

"Rrrubbbishhhh! See that man down there wearing that big coat? I bet I can blow it off him," the Wind boasted.

"Go on then," said the Sun.

The Wind roared and blew as hard as he could. He blew and blew, but the man just held his coat tighter. After a while, the Wind ran out of puff.

"My turn," flashed the Sun. As the Sun smiled, the air got hotter. As it got hotter, the man shrugged off his coat. "There!" twinkled the Sun.

The Wind was so angry he stormed off in a big huff.

22

Story time

Further reading

Read some books retelling other Aesop's fables, for example:

Aesop's Fables for Little Children
Various authors and John Joven (illustrator)

The Orchard Book of Aesop's Fables
retold by Michael Morpurgo
and Emma Chichester Clark (illustrator)

Rhyme time

Encourage the children to repeat this rhyme with you:

> I see the wind when the leaves dance by,
> I see the wind when the clothes wave, "Hi!"
> I see the wind when the trees bend low,
> I see the wind when the flags all blow,
> I see the wind when the kites fly high,
> I see the wind when the clouds float by,
> I see the wind when it blows my hair,
> I see the wind 'most everywhere!

UNIT 11: Reading comprehension lesson

3. Comprehension activities

Look at Student Book page 23 with the class. Tell the children to:

1. Read the sentence and draw a picture.
2. Write inside the outlined text.
3. Complete the yes / no questions by circling the correct answer.
4. Read and answer the questions. Encourage the children to write in complete sentences.

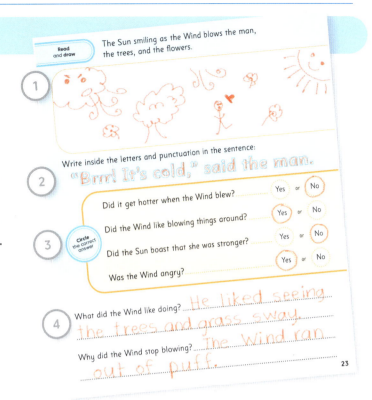

The children can also...
- Find the two words in the story with the <ear> spelling.
- Read the passage with a partner.

 4. Plenary

Read the story again as a class. Encourage the children to read with expression and fluency. Children could be chosen to read the words said by the Wind and the Sun.

Further activities

- Paint pictures showing different types of weather like rain, fog, sun, or snow.
- Discuss what clothes people wear in different weather.
- Find out about the weather in different countries.

Learning objectives

The children are learning to:
- Listen to, discuss, and recall details from different types of writing (play and fable).
- Become familiar with, and retell, traditional stories and rhymes.
- Discuss word meanings, linking new words to those they already know.
- Identify basic similarities or differences between two texts on the same topic (the story in unit 11 and the play in unit 10).

The Wind and the Sun

57

UNIT 11: Writing skills lesson

The Wind and the Sun: a fable

Before class
Cut out the pictures in the Student Book on page 77 to use and reorder for this unit.

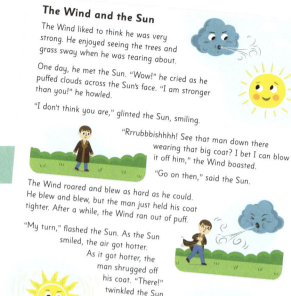

 1. Introductory activity

Remind the children of **The Wind and the Sun** play and story. Remind them that this tale is a special sort of story called a fable, which was written a long time ago by a man called Aesop.

If possible, read the story with the class, using **The Wind and the Sun** (Jolly Phonics Reader, Red Level, General Fiction). If the class requires an e-book of this title, one can be downloaded from https://jollylearning.com/ereader-aep

 2. Talk about the writing

Show the children the pictures and discuss what is happening in each one. Ask the children to point to the pictures in order to show what happens at the beginning, in the middle, and end of the story.

 3. Writing activity

1. Ask the children to suggest a sentence that would be a good start to the story.
2. Choose one of the sentences and model the text by writing it on the board.
3. The children can use this sentence to start writing their own version of the fable.

Encourage the children to write in sentences, think about the words they use, and include lots of details.

The children can also...
- Re-read their own work, ensuring it makes sense.
- Draw a picture to illustrate the story.

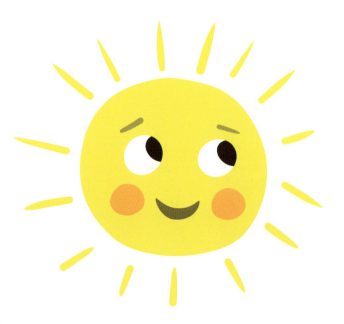

UNIT 11: Writing skills lesson

4. Plenary

Share some of the children's work, either by showing it to the other children or by asking some of them to read out what they have written.

Further activities

- Think of some other words for *wind*. (For example: *breeze, gale, hurricane, tornado, gusts, storm, squall, typhoon,* and *whirlwind*.)
- Think of some other words to describe sunshine or hot things. (For example: *sizzling, roasting, scorching, warm, baking, bright,* and *summery*.)
- Write down each set of words, with the words for *wind* on a cloud shape and the words for *sunshine* or hot things in a yellow circle.

Assessment

The child writes some sentences; most words are plausibly spelled, but with little or no punctuation.		The child writes in sentences for at least one page independently, using periods and correct spellings for most known and regular words; makes plausible attempts at spelling unknown and irregular words; uses knowledge from the story and adds extra information.
The child writes independently, using plausible spellings and some periods; retells the basic story with their writing.		

Learning objectives

The children are learning to:
- Discuss what they are going to write about.
- Understand different types of writing and use images to support their understanding.
- Write simple sentences to create a sequence of events (narrative).
- Write words using phonically plausible spellings.
- Read their own writing aloud to others.

The Wind and the Sun: a fable

Flower farm

UNIT 12: Reading comprehension lesson

 1. Read the story

Read the story to the class. Ensure the children can see the text, pointing to the words as you read. Read the story again, sounding out any difficult or unusual words, such as *field, wanted, colored, daisies, delphiniums,* and *orange*. Check that the children know the meaning of these words. Briefly look at the punctuation, mentioning the speech marks and the exclamation point.

 2. Talk about the story

- Where was the field?
- What did Sally want to do?
- Why did she divide the field into squares?
- What did she plant?
- How did Sally care for the seeds?
- What is a scarecrow for?
- How do you make a scarecrow?
- What did she do with the flowers she grew?

Flower farm

Next to a farmhouse was a big square field. Sally, Farmer Green's wife, stood and looked at the bare area.

Sally wanted to start her own little flower farm there. She prepared the ground and divided it into squares. Then, into each square she planted some different flower seeds. "That will do," she said.

Next, she made a scarecrow and stood it in the middle of the field. "There!" she said.

She cared for the seeds, and by the summer they had all grown so the field was full of squares of different colored flowers. There were yellow sunflowers, white daisies, pink cosmos, purple lavender, blue delphiniums, and orange marigolds.

"A rainbow of flowers," said Sally, as she made them up into colorful bunches to sell at the farmers' market.

24

Story time

Further reading

Read some books about flowers and colors, for example:

Camille and the Sunflowers Laurence Anholt

Sam Plants a Sunflower (National Trust)
Kate Petty (author) and Axel Scheffler (illustrator)

How Do You Make a Rainbow?
Caroline Crowe (author) and
Cally Johnson-Isaacs (illustrator)

Red Rockets and Rainbow Jelly Sue Heap and Nick Sharratt

The Color Monster Anna Llenas

The Rainbow (Jolly Plays) Louise Van-Pottelsberghe

Rhyme time

Encourage the children to repeat this rhyme with you:

> *Roses are red,*
> *Violets are blue,*
> *Sugar is sweet*
> *And so are you.*

60

UNIT 12: Reading comprehension lesson

Flower farm

3. Comprehension activities

Look at Student Book page 25 with the class. Tell the children to:

1. Read the phrases and draw a picture for each one.
2. Complete the yes / no questions by circling the correct answer.
3. Read and answer the questions. Encourage the children to write complete sentences.

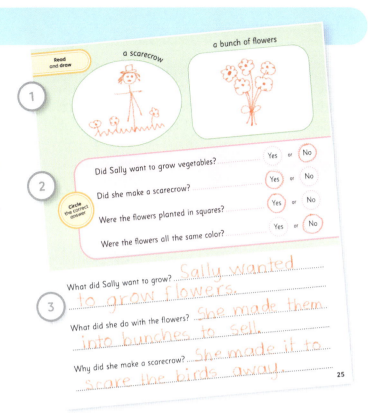

> **The children can also...**
> - Find out about different flowers.
> - Look at, and collect, different words for colors, such as *turquoise, emerald,* and *scarlet*.
> - Draw or use sticky paper squares to make a colorful pattern or picture.

 4. Plenary

Read the story again as a class. Encourage the children to use the punctuation to help them read with expression and fluency. Ask some children what their favorite color is and why.

 Further activities

- Draw, or paint, bunches of flowers.
- Look at some famous flower paintings such as Vincent Van Gogh's **Sunflowers** or Claude Monet's **Water Lilies**.
- Do some color mixing and try adding black and white paints to different colors.
- Plant some flower seeds and care for them.

Learning objectives

The children are learning to:
- Listen to, discuss, and recall details from story texts.
- Link what they hear or read to their own experiences.
- Discuss word meanings, linking new words to those they already know.
- Use inference.
- Appreciate rhymes and poems, and recite some by heart.

UNIT 12: Writing skills lesson

Colors

1. Introductory activity

Revise the words for different colors. Discuss various colors and the names for colors, such as *sky blue, sunshine yellow,* and *bright white.* If possible, get some paint charts and look at the color names on them. Discuss how different colors make the children think or feel; blue for sad or cold, and red for hot or danger, for example.

2. Talk about the writing

Ask the children what things are usually a particular color, for example: fire engines are red, the sky is blue, and the grass is green. Divide the class into groups and give each group a color. Each group should think of as many things of that color as possible. The children can write, or draw, the things on a sheet of paper or in a color splat of that color. Each group then tells the rest of the class all the things noted as being of that color.

3. Writing activity

1. Tell the children that they are going to write a color poem, comparing colors to different things.

2. Explain to the children that colors can be used to describe things and to make writing more interesting; for example, something is not just described as black, but black as coal. Also, there is a wide range in colors, so blue can mean anything from very pale light blue through to dark blue or navy.

3. Tell them that comparing a color to something else tells the actual tone of color more exactly. Similes compare one thing to another. For example:

   Green as grass,
   Green as trees,
   Green as leaves,
   Green as peas,
   Green as a caterpillar!

Explain that...

- Poems have lines and verses, and although the words at the end of the lines often rhyme, they don't have to.

The children can also...

- Re-read their work, ensuring it makes sense.
- Write the words for the different colors in the stripes of a rainbow. For example, the word *red* in a red pen in the top stripe, *orange* in the next stripe down, etc.

62

UNIT 12: Writing skills lesson

Colors

 4. Plenary

Share some of the children's work. Ask a few of the children to read out what they have written for a particular color.

Further activities

- Paint a picture entirely in one color.
- Create a color chart or graph of favorite colors.
- Look at artists who only use a few colors in their work such as Piet Mondrian, Vincent Van Gogh, or Mark Rothko.

 Assessment

The child knows and can identify colors and can write regular color words such as *red*, and attempts to write others such as *orange*, as well as a word or phrase or each color; may need support to think of things of that color and to sound out words.

The child knows and can identify colors and can think of things that are a particular color; can spell color words and writes independently several phrases for each color, with correct spellings for known and regular words; makes plausible attempts at spelling unknown and irregular words.

The child knows and can identify colors and think of things that are a particular color; can spell most color words as well as write independently a phrase for each color, using plausible spellings.

Learning objectives

The children are learning to:
- Discuss what they are going to write about.
- Understand they are comparing a color to a particular thing.
- Use a simple plan to support or organize writing.
- Spell color words and use similes.
- Write words using phonically plausible spelling.
- Re-read their work, ensuring it makes sense.

63

UNIT 13: Reading comprehension lesson

Grandpa's party

 1. Read the story

Read the story to the class. Ensure the children can see the text, pointing to the words as you read. Read the story again, sounding out any difficult or unusual words, such as *barbecue, umbrella, fantastic,* and *chuckled.* Check that the children know the meaning of these words. Point out capital letters and punctuation, such as periods, speech marks, and exclamation points.

 2. Talk about the story

- Who was the party for?
- What sort of food did they have?
- What was the weather like?
- How did they stop the food getting wet?
- What games do you think they played at the party?
- Did Grandpa enjoy the party?
- What sort of food do you and your family eat at parties?
- Talk about families and family members. (For example: *aunt, uncle, niece, brother, sister.*)

The children can also...
- Talk about, and write out, the different names given for their grandparents, aunts, and uncles in places around the world and in different nationalities.
- Create a classroom display of these names.

Grandpa's party

Holly's grandfather was having a party.

On Saturday morning, Holly helped lay out the food and set up a big red tent and some games in the garden. All the family were coming to the party.

By lunchtime, everyone was very hungry. Holly's dad was cooking food on the barbecue. Suddenly it started to rain.

"Quickly!" shouted Holly's dad. "Bring me an umbrella. The food is getting wet."

Uncle Jimmy ran over and held an umbrella over the barbecue.

After lunch, the rain stopped, so they could leave the tent and play all the games outside.

That evening, Grandpa was very happy. "I did enjoy my party," he said. "It was a really fantastic day, even if it was a bit wet," he chuckled.

26

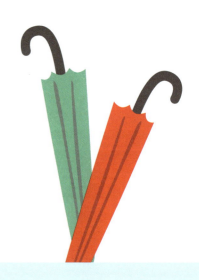

Story time

Further reading

Read books about families and parties, for example:

Love Makes a Family Sophie Beer

The Birthday Party Helen Oxenbury

Big Beach BBQ Carly Taylor (author) and Vaughan Duck (illustrator)

Rhyme time

Encourage the children to repeat this rhyme with you:

Happy birthday to you!
Happy birthday to you!
Happy birthday, dear (name)*,*
Happy birthday to you.

64

UNIT 13: Reading comprehension lesson

Grandpa's party

3. Comprehension activities

Look at Student Book page 27 with the class. Tell the children to:

1. Read the phrases and draw a picture for each one.
2. Write inside the outlined text.
3. Complete the yes / no questions by circling the correct answer.
4. Read and answer the questions. Encourage the children to write in complete sentences.

The children can also...
- Find all the words with a <y> at the end saying /ee/.
- Read the story with a partner.
- Draw a picture of the party.

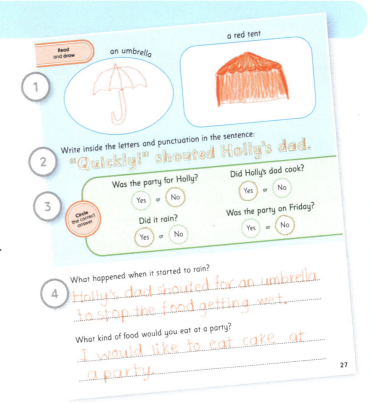

4. Plenary

Read the story again as a class. Encourage the children to read with expression and fluency.

➤➤ Further activities

- Make a list of some of the words used for members of a family. (For example: *uncle, aunt, niece, cousin*.)
- Suggest that the children talk to their uncles, aunts, or grandparents about when they were young.
- Find out about different celebrations around the world.

Learning objectives

The children are learning to:
- Listen to, discuss, and recall details from story texts.
- Link what they hear or read to their own experiences.
- Discuss word meanings, linking new words to those they already know.
- Recite rhymes by heart.

UNIT 13: Writing skills lesson

Parties and invitations

Before class
Gather examples of different invitations either in paper form or print some from the internet.

 ## 1. Introductory activity

Talk about families with the class, including extended families. Talk about the names used for family members (for example: *aunt, niece, uncle, cousin, brother,* and *sister*) and those around the world and with different nationalities. Discuss characteristics that describe people, such as being nice, kind, old, young, fun, clever. Encourage the children to describe more than just physical characteristics.

 ## 2. Talk about the writing

Talk about parties and celebrations that families have and what food they might eat. Look at invitations and discuss the information an invite needs. (*Date, time, place, who or what the party is celebrating.*) Pick out some proper nouns and remind the class that these nouns have capital letters because they are the names of people and things, such as streets, towns, countries, days, months, and buildings.

Point out...
...the letters RSVP. Explain that they stand for *répondez s'il vous plaît*, which is French for *please respond*. Why do people need to reply to an invitation?

 ## 3. Writing activity

1. Tell the children they are going to design and write their own invitation.

2. Ask them to suggest what the invitation could be for – perhaps a birthday party, anniversary, wedding, family party, Diwali celebration, Halloween, or Christmas party.

3. Discuss what things they will need to include on the invitation—what or who is it for, where will it take place, what time does it start and finish? Does it have an RSVP?

4. Ask them how they might decorate the invitation for the different events.

5. Then, ask the children to imagine that they were at the party and write about being there. Who was invited? What did they do or play? What did they eat?

The children can also...
- Decorate the invitation to reflect the type of party.
- Re-read their work, ensuring it makes sense.

UNIT 13: Writing skills lesson

 Parties and invitations

👥 4. Plenary

Share some of the children's work, either by showing it to the other children or by asking some of them to read out what they have written.

➡️ Further activities

- Draw a family picture and write the names of everyone underneath.
- Write a menu for a party or celebration.
- Write, or draw, a list of things that would be needed for a party.
- Play some party games in the classroom together.

⭐ Assessment

The child fills in the invitation; can talk about what happened at the party; writes some words or sentences using phonically plausible spelling but with little or no punctuation.

The child correctly fills in the invitation and decorates it appropriately; writes most of one page independently about what happened at the party, using phonically plausible spellings and some periods and capital letters.

The child correctly fills in the invitation and decorates it appropriately; writes in sentences for at least one page independently about what happened at the party, using periods, capital letters, and correct spellings for most known and regular words; makes plausible attempts at spelling irregular and unknown words.

Learning objectives

The children are learning to:
- Discuss what they are going to write about.
- Understand different types of writing (invitations).
- Say a sentence.
- Write simple sentences.
- Fill in a form (invitation), with support.
- Re-read their writing to check that it makes sense.

67

UNIT 14: Reading comprehension lesson

A thank-you cake

 ## 1. Read the story

Read the story to the class. Ensure the children can see the text, pointing to the words as you read. Read the story again, sounding out any difficult or unusual words, such as *sidewalk* and *ginger*. Check that the children know the meaning of these words.

 ## 2. Talk about the story

- What was the weather like?
- Who did Jane see?
- What happened to Mrs Baker?
- Why did Mrs Baker bring a cake round?
- Why did Mrs Baker decorate the cake with stars?
- What flavor was the cake?
- What flavor cakes do the children like?
- Why does Mrs Baker say there was something good about falling over? (*Since falling over, Mrs Baker visits Jane and her mom more often.*)

A thank-you cake

Jane lives next door to old Mrs Baker. One rainy evening, Jane looked out of her window and saw Mrs Baker trip on the sidewalk and fall over. Jane shouted for her mom and they ran out to help.

The next day, they went to see Mrs Baker and took her a bunch of grapes. She had a cut on her nose and a black eye.

The next weekend, Mrs Baker came round carrying a huge ginger cake with Jane's name on it.

"I made it for you and used chocolate stars to decorate it," said Mrs Baker, "because you were such a star for helping me."

Now, Mrs Baker often visits Jane and her mom, and brings them cakes.

"I enjoy visiting. I'm glad something good came out of my fall," she said, and smiled.

28

Story time

Further reading

Read some stories and books about food and cooking, and look at some cake recipe books, for example:

Cheese Stars Jolly Phonics Reader, Yellow Level, Nonfiction

Gruffalo Crumble and Other Recipes
Julia Donaldson (author) and Axel Scheffler (illustrator)

My First Cookbook
Annabel Karmel (author) and Alex Willmore (illustrator)

The Best Ever Baking Book Jane Bull

Rhyme time

Encourage the children to sing this rhyme with you to the tune of **Here we go round the mulberry bush**:

This is the way we mix a cake, mix a cake, mix a cake,*
This is the way we mix a cake, on a cold and frosty morning.

* Repeat verse using these words:
This is the way we cook the cake...
This is the way we ice the cake...
This is the way we cut the cake...
This is the way we eat the cake...

68

UNIT 14: Reading comprehension lesson

3. Comprehension activities

Look at Student Book page 29 with the class. Tell the children to:

1. Read the phrases and draw a picture for each one.
2. Complete the yes / no questions by circling the correct answer.
3. Read and answer the questions. Encourage the children to write a complete sentence.

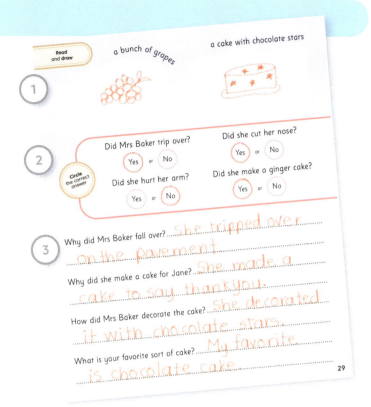

The children can also...
- Find all the words in the story with split digraph spellings, like ‹a-e›.
- Read the story with a partner.
- Write a sentence from the story and draw a picture to illustrate it.

4. Plenary

Read the story again as a class. Ask some children how they answered the questions.

Further activities

- Look at some recipe books together.
- Make a display of different shaped cake tins.
- Make some cakes with different flavorings and see if the children can identify the flavors.

Learning objectives

The children are learning to:
- Listen to, discuss, and recall details from fiction and nonfiction.
- Link what is read or heard to their own experiences.
- Discuss word meanings, linking new words to those they already know.
- Use images to support their understanding of the text.
- Recite rhymes by heart.

A thank-you cake

UNIT 14: Writing skills lesson

Cake recipe

Before class
Find, and photocopy, some recipes for baking cakes or use the recipe on this page. You could also cut up the pictures in the Student Book on page 79 to use and reorder for this unit.

 1. Introductory activity

Ask if the children remember the story **A thank-you cake**. Why did Mrs Baker make a thank-you cake? Talk about cakes: What different sorts of cakes can the children think of? What is their favorite type of cake? Have any of the children made cakes and who with? What sort of cake did they make? How was the cake decorated?

To make a simple cake, or cup cakes:
- 3.5 ounces soft butter
- 3.5 ounces sugar
- 2 eggs
- 3.5 ounces self-raising flour
- 1 teaspoon baking powder
- 1/2 teaspoon of vanilla essence

– Turn the oven on to 400°F (200°C) and let it heat up.
– Using scales, weigh the margarine and put it into a big bowl. Then, weigh the sugar and flour and add that to the bowl too.
– Sprinkle in the baking powder.
– Break in the eggs and stir all the ingredients until the mixture is smooth.
– Use cupcake cases or line a cake tin with a greaseproof liner.
– Spoon the mixture into the cases or tin and bake in the oven for 15-20 minutes or until the cake(s) are golden brown.
– Leave the cakes to cool.

 2. Talk about the writing

How did any of the children who have baked a cake know what to do? Discuss recipes, which give the instructions to make something to eat, such as a cake. Look at **Cheese Stars** (Jolly Phonics, Yellow Reader, Nonfiction), if the class requires an e-book of this title, one can be downloaded from https://jollylearning.com/ereader-aep, or use the recipe above.

Point out that there are lots of verbs in a recipe: *cut, mix, stir, beat, chop,* for example.

Recipes begin with a list of ingredients specifying how much of each item is required. After the ingredient list, a recipe tells people what to do, giving one step at a time in the correct order.

Look at the stages for cake making, pointing out the ingredients. Sound out and write some words relevant to these visual prompts on the board. Discuss how ingredients are measured: in cups, spoons, and grams or ounces.

 3. Writing activity

1. The children are going to write their own recipe for making a cake. They can use the recipe example or use the pictures in the Student Book to help them with the ingredients.

2. Have the children, either individually or in pairs or groups, sort out and reorder the cut up pieces of the recipe you give them.

3. Then the children write the recipe themselves, saying what the cook needs to do at each step to make the cake.

The children can also...
- Think of ways in which they can decorate cakes.
- Draw pictures of their cakes.
- Talk about a cake they would like to create—what flavor would it be and how would they decorate it.

UNIT 14: Writing skills lesson

 4. Plenary

Share some of the children's work, either by showing it to the other children or by asking some of them to read out what they have written.

 Further activities

- Draw a bar graph of favorite cake flavors.
- Talk about allergies.
- Write a menu, or set of labels, for a cake shop and decorate them.

 Assessment

The child attempts to write words or sentences for each stage using plausible spellings but little or no punctuation; understands that a recipe is a set of instructions and orders the pictures and instructions correctly, possibly with some help.

The child writes independently using plausible spellings with some punctuation, periods and capital letters; understands that a recipe is a set of instructions, and orders the pictures and instructions correctly, writing something for each stage of the recipe and using the pictures to help.

The child writes independently in sentences for more than a page, using periods, capital letters, and correct spellings for most known and regular words; makes plausible attempts at spelling unknown and irregular words; understands that a recipe is a set of instructions; orders the pictures and instructions correctly without help and writes something for each stage of the recipe, using the pictures to help and also adding some instructions or ideas of their own.

Learning objectives

The children are learning to:
- Discuss what they are going to write about.
- Understand different types of writing.
- Use a simple plan (a recipe) to support or organize writing.
- Write simple sentences.
- Write words using phonically plausible spellings.
- Re-read their writing, ensuring it makes sense.
- Read their writing aloud to others.

Anansi the spider and the melon

 1. Read the folktale

Read the story to the class. Ensure the children can see the text, pointing to the words as you read. Read the story again, sounding out any difficult or unusual words, such as *melon, Hey!, gasped,* and *excuse.* Check that the children know the meaning of these words.

Explain that...

...Anansi the spider is a character from West African folklore. Anansi is also called the trickster because he likes to play tricks and jokes on people. He features in a number of fables from Ghana and the Ashanti people.

Anansi the spider and the melon

One morning, Anansi the spider made a hole in Goat's prize melon with a thorny spike. The spider squeezed inside and ate as much of the melon as he could. But when it was time to climb out he was stuck!

"I'll have to stay," he smiled.

The next day, Goat picked the melon. "Hey!" shouted Anansi.

"Wow, a talking melon!" gasped Goat. "I must take it to the king."

The king ordered the melon to speak, but it didn't.

"Silly!" said the king.

"Excuse me!" replied Anansi from inside. "You are the one talking to a melon!"

The king was so cross, he threw the melon out of the window. It smashed and Anansi crawled out. He ran up a tree and hid in a bunch of bananas.

"That's the last time I listen to a melon," cried Goat.

"No, you can never trust a melon," replied a banana.

 2. Talk about the folktale

- What sort of animal is Anansi?
- Who did the melon belong to?
- How did Anansi get inside the melon?
- Why could Anansi not get out of the melon?
- Why did Anansi smile when he said he would have to stay inside the melon?

- Why did Goat take the melon to the king?
- What did the king order the melon to do?
- What did the melon do?
- Why was the king cross with the melon?
- Did the banana really speak?

Story time

Further reading

Read some other stories and books about Anansi or spiders, for example:

Anansi's Narrow Waist H. J. Arrington (author) and Nicole Allin (illustrator)

The Very Busy Spider Eric Carle

Spinderella Julia Donaldson (author) and Sebastien Braun (illustrator)

Rhyme time

This is one of Anansi's favorite rhymes because it has a trick in it! Encourage the children to repeat this with you:

*As I was going to St Ives,
I met a man with seven wives,
Each wife had seven sacks,
Each sack had seven cats,
Each cat had seven kittens,
Kits, cats, sacks, and wives,
How many were going to St Ives?*

(The answer is only one person – the narrator.)

UNIT 15: Reading comprehension lesson

72

UNIT 15: Reading comprehension lesson

3. Comprehension activities

Look at Student Book page 31 with the class. Tell the children to:

1. Read the phrases and draw a picture for each one.
2. Complete the yes / no questions by circling the correct answer.
3. Read and answer the questions. Encourage the children to write in complete sentences.

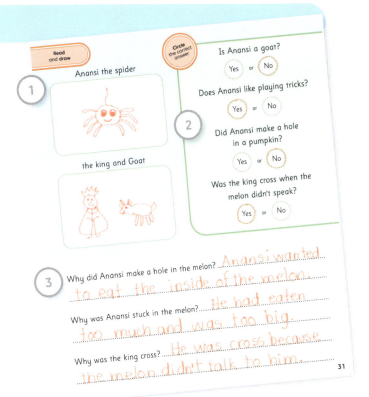

The children can also...
- Find all the words in the story with a split digraph spelling, like <i-e>.
- Underline the verbs in red.
- Compare their work with that of a partner.

 ### 4. Plenary

Read the story again as a class, using the punctuation to help read with expression and fluency. Different children could be chosen to read Anansi, Goat, and the king. Ask some of the children how they answered the questions.

 ### Further activities

- Find out about spiders.
- Read or perform **Why Anansi the Spider has Eight Thin Legs** (Jolly Plays).
- Find out about Ghana and West Africa, where many Anansi stories originate.

Learning objectives

The children are learning to:
- Listen to, discuss, and recall details from story texts.
- Become familiar with, and retell, traditional stories and rhymes.
- Discuss the significance of the title and events in the story.
- Use inference.

UNIT 15: Writing skills lesson

Anansi the spider

Before class
Ensure every child has access to a copy of the picture in the Student Book.

1. Introductory activity

Remind the class about the story of **Anansi and the talking melon**. Ask the children what happened at the beginning, middle, and end of the story. Ask what tricks Anansi played and what were the funny bits of the story.

2. Talk about the writing

With the class, look at the picture and find Anansi. Discuss how he might reach the melon.
(For example: *by crawling down the tree, dropping on a thread, running along the ground, over vegetables, then under leaves*.)

- How did Anansi make the hole in the melon?
- Where might Anansi have found the spike or the thorn?
- Was it difficult for Anansi to make the hole?
- What do the children think it felt like inside the melon?
- What did the melon taste like?
- How did Goat feel when he heard the melon talking?
- How did Anansi feel when the melon smashed on the ground?
- Why did Anansi run up the tree and hide in the bunch of bananas?

3. Writing activity

1. Draw a picture to show the route Anansi took to reach the melon.
2. Continue to plan the story by drawing pictures for each scene.
3. Write the story using the pictures to help.

The children can also...
- Re-read their work, ensuring it makes sense.
- Read some other stories about Anansi.

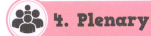

UNIT 15: Writing skills lesson

Anansi the spider

4. Plenary

Share some of the children's work, either by showing it to the other children or by asking some of them to read out what they have written.

Further activities

- Draw or paint a picture of Anansi the spider.
- Try retelling the story pretending to be Anansi.
- Find out more about spiders.

Assessment

The child writes some sentences using plausible spellings of most words but little or no punctuation; uses some ideas from the picture in their writing.

The child writes independently some sentences for at least a page using plausible spellings of most words; uses some ideas from the picture and retells the basic story in their writing.

The child writes one or two pages independently, mostly in sentences with periods and correct spellings of most known and regular words; makes plausible attempts at spelling irregular and unknown words; uses some ideas from the picture and knowledge from the story as well as adding extra information to their writing.

Learning objectives

The children are learning to:
- Discuss what they are going to write about.
- Use a simple plan (story map) to support or organize their writing.
- Write simple sentences to create a sequence of events (narrative).
- Use speech marks.
- Write words using phonically plausible spellings.
- Re-read their work, ensuring it makes sense.

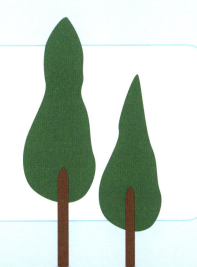

UNIT 16: Reading comprehension lesson

Globes

📖 1. Read the text

Read the passage to the class. Ensure the children can see the text, pointing to the words as you read. Read the passage again, sounding out any difficult or unusual words, such as *sphere, globe, planet, countries, Earth,* and *rotates.* Check that the children know the meaning of these words.

2. Talk about the text

- What is a globe?
- What shape is a globe?
- What does a globe show?
- Why does the word *Earth* have a capital letter?
- Why does a globe rotate?
- How did people long ago show the areas that were not known?
- Why did they put imaginary animals and sea monsters on unknown parts?
- What animal would you draw to show particular places? *(India could show a snake, elephant, or tiger; China might have a panda, etc.)*
- Why might a globe be better than a map?

Story time

Further reading

Look at some maps and atlases and read some books about explorers or dragons, for example:

Adventures around the Globe
Lonely Planet Kids

Here Be Dragons Susannah Lloyd (author) and Paddy Donnelly (illustrator)

The Great Explorer Chris Judge

Famous Explorers Joshua George (author) and Ed Myer (illustrator)

Captain Scott Jolly Phonics Reader, Green Level, Nonfiction

Rhyme time

Encourage the children to repeat this rhyme with you:

> *I'm glad the sky is painted blue,*
> *And the Earth is painted green,*
> *With such a lot of nice fresh air*
> *All sandwiched in between.*

UNIT 16: Reading comprehension lesson

 3. Comprehension activities

Look at Student Book page 33 with the class. Tell the children to:

1. Read the phrases and draw a picture for each one.

2. Complete the yes / no questions by circling the correct answer.

3. Read and answer the questions. Encourage the children to write a complete sentence.

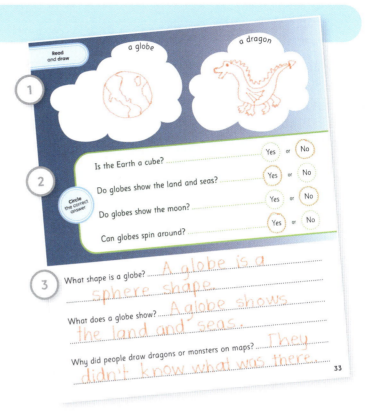

The children can also...

- Read the passage with a partner.
- Find all the words in the text with a /o-e/ sound.
- Find all the words in the text with an <o-e> spelling.
- Underline nouns with a black pencil and verbs with a red pencil.
- Compare their work with that of a partner.

 4. Plenary

Read the passage again as a class. Encourage the children to read with expression and fluency. Ask some of the children how they answered the questions.

 Further activities

- Look at a globe.
- Look at maps and atlases.
- Draw, or paint, a picture of land and seas on a circle of paper.
- Draw, or paint, a sea monster or dragon.
- Look at, or read, books about explorers.

Learning objectives

The children are learning to:
- Listen to, discuss, and recall details from nonfiction.
- Link what they read or hear to their own experiences.
- Discuss the facts they extract from the text.
- Recite rhymes by heart.

UNIT 16: Writing skills lesson

Yesteryear

1. Introductory activity

Briefly discuss globes, maps, and exploring the world. Remind the children that in the past, people living in different places did not know anything about each other, other countries, or the different animals that lived there. People would go on expeditions to unexplored places to find out about them. When they came back, they would either bring things with them or try and describe the strange things and unfamiliar animals they had seen. People would try and draw these animals from the descriptions. As they had never actually seen the animals this sometimes led to some very strange pictures, as in the picture of the elephant in the Student Book and below.

2. Talk about the writing

Look at, and discuss, the picture of the elephant. While the children have seen pictures of elephants, and possibly seen real elephants, people in the past had not. They knew elephants existed, and had heard, or read, descriptions of them. If they wanted to draw a picture of an elephant, they had to use those descriptions and their imaginations. Ask the children if they think the picture looks like an elephant. Ask which parts they think are accurate and which are not.

Read them the following description and ask them to draw a picture of the animal. You can tell them before or after they draw that it is a description of a numbat.

This creature is: a small furry animal that is mostly a reddish-brown color, but with black and white stripes across its back. Its back legs are shorter than its front legs and it has a long, fluffy tail, a bit like a squirrel. It has a long, thin snout and a long, pink tongue. It has black eyes and a black nose, with thin, upright ears. There is a black stripe running from its ears to its nose.

Ask the children to show their drawings and to compare them. Look at a picture of a numbat together. Do they think their drawing looks like it?

Digital images courtesy of Getty's Open Content Program.

3. Writing activity

The children think of an animal or bird and write a description of it. Alternatively, they could find a picture of a strange or exotic creature and write a description based on the picture, either in small groups or individually.

A creature to describe could be: an armadillo, an aardvark, a pangolin, a giant anteater, a tenrec, a nudibranch, a shoebill, or a hoatzin.

UNIT 16: Writing skills lesson

 4. Plenary

Ask some children to read their description and see if the other children can guess what the animal is or can pick it out from a selection of pictures.

 Further activities

- Find out about some strange and exotic creatures.
- Find some more pictures of animals that were drawn in the past to show the children.
- Make a display with the descriptions and pictures of the creatures. The children can see if they can identify the creature from the description and match it to the correct picture.

Assessment

The child writes some words, most of which are plausibly spelled but with little or no punctuation; directly observes and identifies a few of the animal's characteristics.

The child writes at least a page independently, using plausible spellings and some periods; directly observes and identifies most of the animal's characteristics.

The child writes independently at least one or two pages in sentences, using periods and with correct spellings of most known and regular words; makes plausible attempts at spelling unknown and irregular words; directly observes and identifies the animal's characteristics and writes a description from which the animal can be recognized.

Learning objectives

The children are learning to:
- Discuss what they are going to write about.
- Observe and identify physical characteristics in a picture.
- Write simple sentences to form a description.
- Write words using phonically plausible spelling.
- Re-read their work, ensuring it makes sense.
- Read and discuss their own writing with others.

Boat trip

UNIT 17: Reading comprehension lesson

 1. Read the story

Read the story to the class. Ensure the children can see the text, pointing to the words as you read. Read the story again, sounding out any difficult or unusual words, such as *cameras, appear, disappearing,* and *photographs*. Check that the children know the meaning of these words. Briefly look at the punctuation, mentioning the speech marks as well as the exclamation points.

 2. Talk about the story

- What were the children doing?
- Who is the captain of the boat?
- What does a captain do?
- What did they see?
- What did the dolphins do?
- Did the children enjoy themselves?
- Why does Amara think dolphins look happy?
- What does Amara like to do?

Story time

Further reading

Read some stories and books about dolphins, for example:

Daisy the Dolphin Natalie Pritchard (author) and Natalie Merheb (illustrator)

Dolphin Boy Michael Morpurgo (author) and Michael Foreman (illustrator)

Everything Dolphins National Geographic Kids

Ally the Dolphin Fair Daisy Meadows (author)

Rhyme time

Encourage the children to learn this rhyme with you:

> I went in a boat,
> across the sea*.
> To see what I could see.
>
> What did I see?
>
> I saw three dolphins
> Swimming along.
> and smiling happily.

* Try doing hand movements for *sea* (make a wavy motion with hands) and *see* (put hands over eyes).

80

UNIT 17: Reading comprehension lesson

3. Comprehension activities

Look at Student Book page 35 with the class. Tell the children to:

1. Read the phrases and draw a picture for each one.
2. Complete the yes / no questions by circling the correct answer.
3. Read and answer the questions. Encourage the children to write in complete sentences.

> **The children can also...**
> - Find out about dolphins.
> - Think about what makes them happy and discuss with a partner.

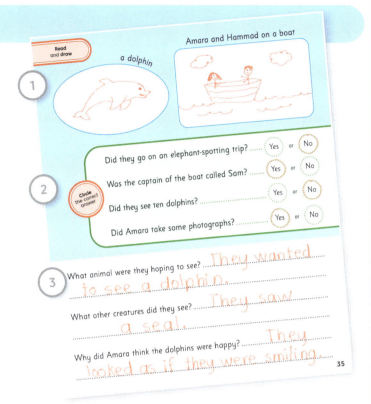

 4. Plenary

Read the story again as a class. Encourage the children to use the punctuation to help them read with expression and fluency. Ask some children what their favorite animal is and why.

 Further activities

- Paint an underwater picture.
- Draw a picture of a dolphin and label it.
- Find out about different types of sea birds.
- Make a graph of their favorite animals.

Learning objectives

The children are learning to:
- Listen to, discuss, and recall details from stories.
- Link what is read or heard to their own experiences.
- Discuss word meanings, linking new words to those they already know.
- Use inference and prediction.
- Recite rhymes by heart.

Boat trip

81

UNIT 17: Writing skills lesson

Happy and sad

1. Introductory activity

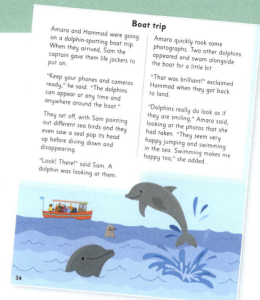

Remind the children about the story of Amara and Hammad's boat trip.

Ask why the children thought the dolphins looked happy. *(They thought the dolphins looked as if they were smiling.)* What does Amara like to do that makes her happy? *(She likes swimming.)*

Explain that the feeling of being happy, or happiness, is an emotion. Our emotions are how we feel. Ask the children to name some other emotions. (For example: *sadness, jealousy, fear, joy, anger*.) Ask them to try to show the emotions using their face; for example, smile to show they are happy, "cry" to show they are sad, frown to show they are angry. Talk about emojis that they see on phone messages and emails. Show some emoji faces and ask what emotions they represent.

2. Talk about the writing

- Ask what makes the children feel happy.
- Ask what makes the children feel sad.
- Explain that sometimes doing something nice for someone else can make them feel happy, as well as the other person.
- In pairs, or groups, ask the children to suggest things they do that make other people happy and what they could do to make the school or class a happier place.
- Ask some children to share their ideas.

3. Writing activity

1. The children can write about what makes them feel happy or sad, then they can write acrostic poems about feelings and what makes them feel different emotions.

2. To write an acrostic poem they start by writing the letters for the word (for example, *happy*) down the left side of the page.

3. They then have to think of things that make them happy beginning with those letters and write them on that line. For example:

   Hugs from my family　　　　**H**ens clucking
   And singing happy songs　　**A** warm sunny day
   Playing with my friends　　　**P**izza on a plate
   Painting a picture of a　　　　**P**uddles in the rain
   Yellow smiling sun　　　　　 **Y**elling as I play

4. They can write out their acrostic poem on a sheet of paper and write over or decorate the initial letter in each line.

UNIT 17: Writing skills lesson

 4. Plenary

Share some of the children's work, either by showing it to the other children or by asking some of them to read out what they have written.

 Further activities

- Paint a happy picture in happy colors.
- Paint a sad picture in sad colors.
- Write a sentence about their happy or sad picture.

 Assessment

The child knows basic emotion words, such as happy, sad, cross, calm, and scared, and attempts to write sentences, using plausible spellings; can think of things that make them feel happy or sad; writes a word beginning with the right letter for an acrostic poem.

The child knows basic emotion words, such as happy, sad, cross, calm, and scared, and writes sentences independently, using plausible spellings; can think of and discuss things that make them feel happy or sad; writes a word beginning with the right letter for an acrostic poem, and can say why it makes them happy or sad.

The child knows basic emotion words, such as happy, sad, cross, calm, and scared, and writes sentences independently using correct spellings for known or regular words; makes plausible attempts at the spelling of unknown or irregular words; can think of and talk about things that make them feel happy or sad; writes a phrase or sentence beginning with the right letter for an acrostic poem, and can say why it makes them happy or sad.

Learning objectives

The children are learning to:
- Discuss what they are going to write about.
- Use a simple plan to support or organize their writing.
- Write simple sentences.
- Write an opinion piece.
- Write words using phonically plausible spellings.
- Re-read their writing to check that it makes sense.

How the whale got his throat

 ## 1. Read the fable

Read the story to the class. Ensure the children can see the text, pointing to the words as you read. Read the story again, sounding out any difficult or unusual words, such as *yummy, shipwrecked, sailor,* and *raft*. Check that the children know the meaning of these words.

 ## 2. Talk about the fable

- What is a whale?
- What did the whale like to do?
- Why was there only one fish left in the sea?
- What does a sailor do?
- What had happened to the sailor?
- What is a raft?
- What did the sailor do when the whale swallowed him?
- What did the sailor want?
- Why could the whale not eat anything except tiny fish from then on?
- What do you think the moral of the story is? (*Don't be greedy.*)

Story time

Further reading

Read some stories and books about whales, for example:

Whales: Safari Readers Tristan Walters

Elmer and the Whales David McKee

The Snail and the Whale Julia Donaldson (author) and Axel Scheffler (illustrator)

Rhyme time

Encourage the children to repeat this rhyme with you:

> *When I was one, I had just begun.*
> *When I was two, I was nearly new.*
> *When I was three, I was hardly me.*
> *When I was four, I was not much more.*
> *When I was five, I was just alive,*
> *But now I am six, I'm as clever as clever,*
> *So I think I'll be six now for ever and ever.*

From the poem **The End** by A. A. Milne.

UNIT 18: Reading comprehension lesson

3. Comprehension activities

Look at Student Book page 37 with the class. Tell the children to:

1. Read the phrases and draw a picture for each one.
2. Complete the yes / no questions by circling the correct answer.
3. Read and answer the questions. Encourage the children to write in complete sentences.

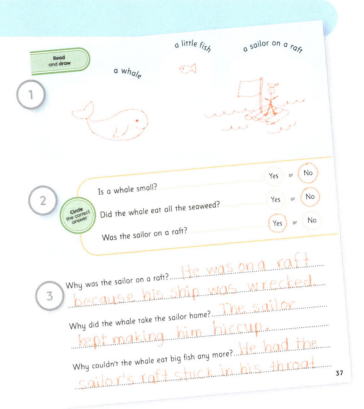

The children can also...
- Find all the words in the story with a <wh> spelling.
- Underline noun words with a black pencil and verbs with a red pencil.
- Compare their work with that of a partner.

 ## 4. Plenary

Read the story again as a class. Encourage the children to read with expression and fluency. Ask some children how they answered the questions.

 Further activities

- Find out about whales.
- Discuss the different jobs people do.
- Look at a globe to find different oceans around the world.

How the whale got his throat

Learning objectives

The children are learning to:
- Listen to, discuss, and recall details from story texts.
- Link what they hear to their own experiences.
- Become familiar with, and retell, traditional stories and rhymes.
- Discuss word meanings, linking new words to those they already know.

UNIT 18: Writing skills lesson

In the future...

1. Introductory activity

Remind the class about the story of **How the whale got his throat**. Talk briefly about what might happen to the sailor after he walks away from the whale. Where does he go? What does he do? Ask the children to finish the sentence in the future tense: When the sailor gets back home, he will... (...have something to eat / tell everyone about what happened / have a bath / stay at home and never go to sea again!)

Talk to the class about what they are looking forward to doing after they leave school today. What would they like to do tomorrow? What do they want to do when they are older?

2. Talk about the writing

Tell the children to think about what they would like to do in the future, when they are grown up.

- What job would they like to do?
- What things do they think will be the same?
- What things do they think will be different?
- Will we learn to look after the environment?
- Will we stop using plastic?
- Will we have a city on the Moon or Mars?
- Will cars be driverless and drive themselves?
- Will we all have robot assistants?

3. Writing activity

Ask the children to write about what they think it will be like in the future and what they would like to do.

> **The children can also...**
> - Re-read their work, ensuring it makes sense.
> - Draw a picture to illustrate their writing

86

UNIT 18: Writing skills lesson

In the future...

 4. Plenary

Share some of the children's work, either by showing it to the other children or by asking some of them to read out what they have written.

 Further activities

- Write a new version of the story **How the whale got his throat**.
- Paint a picture from the story.
- Read some more of Rudyard Kipling's **Just So Stories**.

 Assessment

The child can talk about what might happen in the future and what they might like to do, and their ideas are mostly about themselves; writes some words or sentences using plausible spellings but little or no punctuation.

The child writes about what might happen, what they would like to do and what might be different in the future, and they write mostly about themselves; writes independently more than a page in sentences, using periods and capital letters with correct spellings of most known and regular words; makes plausible attempts at spelling irregular and unknown words.

The child writes about what might happen in the future and what they might like to do, and their ideas are mostly about themselves; attempts to consider what might be different in the future; writes independently at least a page, using plausible spellings and some punctuation, periods and capital letters.

Learning objectives

The children are learning to:
- Discuss what they are going to write about.
- Say a sentence.
- Write simple sentences.
- Write words using phonically plausible spellings.
- Re-read their work, ensuring it makes sense.

87

UNIT 19: Reading comprehension lesson

Book Week

1. Read the story

Read the story to the class. Ensure the children can see the text, pointing to the words as you read. Read the story again, sounding out any difficult or unusual words, such as *excited*, *unicorn*, and *author*. Check that the children know the meaning of these words.

2. Talk about the story

- What was special about the week?
- What were they looking forward to?
- What was happening in the hall?
- What does an author do?
- What is a series?
- Do any children in the class have a favorite author? Or a favorite book?

Story time

Further reading

Read some stories about libraries and book weeks, for example:

Luna Loves Library Day Joseph Coelho (author) and Fiona Lumbers (illustrator)

The Best World Book Week Ever Sarah Oliver (author) and Scott Wells (illustrator)

Lulu Loves the Library Anna McQuinn (author) and Rosalind Beardshaw (illustrator)

Nour's Secret Library Wafa' Tarnowska (author) and Vali Mintzi (illustrator)

Rhyme time

Encourage the children to repeat this rhyme with you:

> We go to the library at least once a week,
> And open the books and take a peek.
> We're hoping as we look around
> Our friend the bookworm can be found.

UNIT 19: Reading comprehension lesson

3. Comprehension activities

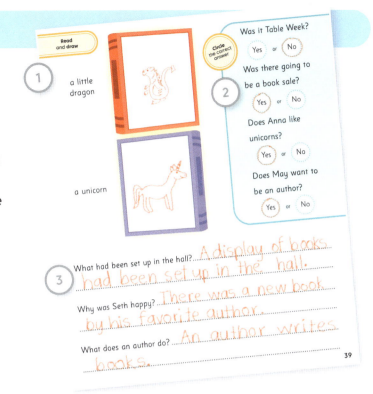

Look at Student Book page 39 with the class. Tell the children to:

1. Read the phrases and draw a picture for each one.
2. Complete the yes / no questions by circling the correct answer.
3. Read and answer the questions. Encourage the children to write in sentences.

The children can also...
- Find all the words in the story with an <ay> spelling.
- Read the passage with a partner.
- Tell their partner about their favorite book.

4. Plenary

Read the text again as a class. Encourage the children to use the punctuation to help them read with expression and fluency.

Further activities

- Make a display of the children's favorite books.
- Look at some books that are part of a series. For example: **The Wombles** (Elisabeth Beresford), **Kipper** (Mick Inkpen) or **Elmer** (David McKee).
- Set a Book Challenge for the children to read a certain number of books in a week.
- Look at and discuss book covers.
- Have each child draw a bookworm, then turn the drawings into bookmarks by mounting them on card.
- Revise the terms *fiction* and *nonfiction* with the children. Sort a selection of books into fiction and nonfiction.

Learning objectives

The children are learning to:
- Listen to, discuss, and recall details from story texts.
- Link what they read or hear to their own experiences.
- Discuss word meanings, linking new words to those they already know.
- Use inference.
- Recite rhymes by heart.

Book Week

89

Book Week

UNIT 19: Writing skills lesson

 1. Introductory activity

Look at, and talk about, books with the class. Explain that the books being looked at in this unit are fiction (or story books) and that nonfiction books do have similar elements.

Show the class that the book titles are in big letters on the front cover. Tell them that the title tells us something about the story. The author is the person who has written the book, and their name is also on the front cover. If it is a book with pictures, then the illustrator (the person who drew the pictures) might also be there.

The picture on the front also tells you something about the story. Look at the back cover of a book (the blurb), which tells you a bit about the book without giving the whole story away. What other information is on the back cover?

 2. Talk about the writing

Choose some books the children have not read. Look at the titles and the images on the front and see if the children can suggest what the story might be about. Some of the books could be read in story time or left out for the children to read, and the readers can find out if they were right about their story suggestions.

Ask the children to suggest titles of stories they know, such as **Jack and the beanstalk**, **Anansi and the talking melon** or some titles of books that have been read in story time. The children can also make up some story titles of their own, perhaps by using some of the words from the spelling lists. For example:

- *The Playground Cat*
- *Whispering Whales*
- *The Play Day*
- *Tadpole Goes Home*

Ask the class to think about, and discuss, what the story might be about for the titles they have thought up.

 3. Writing activity

1. Tell the children to choose a title and design a front cover for the book. They write the title, using big letters, and draw a picture to illustrate a part of the story. They put their own name as the author.

2. For the back cover, they write a few lines about the story. Encourage the children to think about the important parts of the story and tell them to remember not to give away the ending.

The children can also...
- Draw a picture and write a sentence from the story.
- Write the story that goes in the book.
- Re-read their work, ensuring it makes sense.

 4. Plenary

Share some of the children's work, by showing the covers to the rest of the class and asking some of the children to read out what they have written for the back cover.

UNIT 91: Writing skills lesson

Further activities

- Ask the children to give a short talk about their favorite book, focusing on what happens in the story and why they like it.
- Ask the children to find out what their parents' or carer's favorite book was when they were young.
- Visit the school library.
- Arrange a visit to the local library or ask the librarian to visit and talk about the library and books.

Assessment

 The child understands the key features of a fiction book, such as cover, title, author, and illustrator; chooses a title and copies it correctly and draws an appropriate picture; writes something from the story with plausible spellings of most words or phrases but little punctuation.

 The child understands the key features of a fiction book, such as cover, title, author, and illustrator; chooses a title, copies it correctly, and draws an appropriate picture; selects some important parts of the story (enough not to give the end away) and writes some sentences about the story independently, using plausible spellings and some periods.

 The child understands the key features of a fiction book, such as cover, title, author, and illustrator; chooses a title, copies it correctly and draws an appropriate picture; selects some of the main points and most interesting parts of the story and does not give the end away; writes about the story independently in sentences with periods and correct spellings of most known and regular words; makes plausible attempts at spelling unknown and irregular words.

Learning objectives

The children are learning to:
- Discuss what they are going to write about.
- Discuss the key features of a fiction book (front and back cover, title, author, and illustrator).
- Extract information from something they have read.
- Say a sentence.
- Write simple sentences.
- Write words using phonically plausible spellings.
- Re-read their writing to check that it makes sense.

Book Week

91

UNIT 20: Reading comprehension lesson

Characters

📖 1. Read the story

Read the story to the class. Ensure the children can see the text, pointing to the words as you read. Read the story again, sounding out any difficult or unusual words, such as *characters, bowl, scared,* and *chuckled.* Check that the children know the meaning of these words. Look at the punctuation, mentioning the speech marks and exclamation points, particularly after *Kazoom!*

Characters

The children had enjoyed reading lots of stories during Book Week, and today they were each dressed up as characters from stories or rhymes.

Hinda was Miss Muffet with a bowl, teaspoon, and a toy spider. "I really am scared of spiders," she whispered.

Seth was Robin Hood with a toy bow and arrow. "I am brave and strong," he boasted.

Rob was a wizard with a spell book and a wooden wand. He kept pointing the wand and shouting, "Kazoom!"

"ROAR!" Gus cried, as he stomped along. "I am a huge, scary, fire-breathing dragon!"

Anna was Anansi the spider. She had attached six extra-long legs to her T-shirt, giving her eight legs in all. "Look out! I am very tricky," Anna chuckled.

Bill was pretending to be Jack, and he had made a beanstalk from a cane, with green paper leaves and real beans.

40

💬 2. Talk about the story

- What does the word *character* mean?
- Why were the children dressing up?
- Who were the children dressing up as?
- What things did Hinda select to show she was Miss Muffet?
- What things did Rob choose to show he was a wizard?
- Why did Rob shout *Kazoom!*?
- Is *kazoom* a real word?
- Why is the word *ROAR* in capital letters?

Story time

Further reading

Read some stories, books, and series based on a main character, for example:

Thomas the Tank Engine Wilbert and Christopher Awdry

Horrid Henry Francesca Simon (author) and Tony Ross (illustrator)

Captain Underpants Dav Pilkey

The Boy Who Grew / Lived with / Flew with (etc) Dragons Andy Shepherd (author) and Sara Ogilvie (illustrator)

Rhyme time

A limerick is a special type of poem.
It has five lines and is said with a particular rhythm.
Point out that lines 1, 2, and 6 rhyme, as do lines 3 and 4.

> *There once was a man from Bengal,*
> *Who was asked to a fancy-dress ball,*
> *He murmured, "I'll risk it,*
> *And dress as a biscuit",*
> *But a dog ate him up in the hall!*

UNIT 20: Reading comprehension lesson

3. Comprehension activities

Look at Student Book page 41 with the class. Tell the children to:

1. Read the phrases and draw a picture for each one.
2. Complete the yes / no questions by circling the correct answer.
3. Read and answer the questions. Encourage the children to write in sentences.

> **The children can also...**
> - Find words in the story with an <ea> spelling.
> - Read the passage with a partner.
> - Discuss who they would dress up as and what things they would carry or wear to be those characters.

4. Plenary

Read the story again as a class. Encourage the children to use the punctuation to help them read with expression and fluency.

Further activities

- Draw pictures of characters from stories, including items to enable other children to identify the character.
- Watch some cartoons in which the same characters have different adventures.
- Look at a book series in which the same character has different adventures. such as Paddington Bear (Michael Bond), Winnie-the-Pooh (A. A. Milne), and Peter Rabbit (Beatrix Potter).

Learning objectives

The children are learning to:
- Listen to, discuss, and recall details from story texts.
- Discuss word meanings, linking new words to those they already know.
- Talk about the key features of a book, including its title and characters.
- Appreciate different types of rhymes and poems, and recite some by heart.

UNIT 20: Writing skills lesson

Characters

Before class
Find some copies of books, which feature well-known characters and some with the same character appearing in several books in the same series.

1. Introductory activity

Discuss some of the characters from books the children have talked about. These characters are from fiction books, so they are imaginary stories. Sometimes a fictional character, such as Robin Hood, is based on someone that might have been real, but no one really knows, so we assume the stories about them have also been made up. Look at some books the children are familiar with and ask the class who the main characters are in each story.

2. Talk about the writing

Tell the children to think of their favorite character from a story. Ask them to name their favorites and find out why the children like these particular characters. Choose some of the characters and ask the class to think of words to describe their choice. Ask the children what clothing or items each character has that help people identify them. (For example: *Robin Hood has a bow, arrow, and a green felt cap, while Paddington Bear has a red hat, a blue duffle coat, and a marmalade sandwich*.)

3. Writing activity

1. The children choose their favorite character from a story and draw a quick picture of that character.
2. They think of some adjectives to describe the character and write these around the drawing.
3. They write some sentences about the character, describing what they look like, what they are like, and what things they wear, have, or carry.

The children can also...
- Draw a picture and write a sentence from the story.
- Re-read their work, ensuring it makes sense.
- Read and discuss their work with a partner.

4. Plenary

Share some of the children's work by showing the pictures to the other children and asking them to read out what they have written. Alternatively, read some of the children's descriptions to the class but without giving the character's name, and see if the other children can guess the character.

UNIT 20: Writing skills lesson

 Further activities

- Make a character gallery of the children's pictures.
- Have a day when the children dress up as characters from stories.

- Ask the children to bring in a book featuring a character they like and tell the class about the character and why they like them.

 Assessment

The child thinks of a character from a story and draws a picture that can be identified as that character; writes sentences about the character, with some punctuation and correct spellings of some regular and known words; makes plausible attempts at spelling unknown and irregular words; understands the terms *fiction* and *nonfiction*.

The child thinks of a character from a story and draws a picture that can be identified as that character; writes independently at least a page about the character, using some periods and correct spellings of some known and regular words; makes plausible attempts at spelling unknown and irregular words; understands the terms *fiction* and *nonfiction*.

The child thinks of a character from a story and draws a picture that can be identified as that character; writes independently more than a page in sentences about the character, using knowledge from the story and adding extra information; uses periods and correct spellings for most known and regular words; makes plausible attempts at spelling unknown and irregular words; understands the terms *fiction* and *nonfiction*.

Learning objectives

The children are learning to:
- Discuss what they are going to write about.
- Understand what is fiction and nonfiction.
- Identify key features of a story (characters).
- Write simple descriptive sentences.
- Write words using phonically plausible spellings.
- Re-read their writing to check that it makes sense.

UNIT 21: Reading comprehension lesson

The night sky

 1. Read the story

Read the story to the class. Ensure the children can see the text, pointing to the words as you read. Read the story again, sounding out any difficult or unusual words, such as *people, thought, constellations,* and *atmosphere.* Check that the children know the meaning of these words. Briefly look at the punctuation and point out the speech marks and the exclamation point.

 2. Talk about the story

Discuss whether the children have looked at stars or seen a shooting star.

- Who was looking at the stars in the story?
- Why did they go somewhere where it was dark?
- What did people used to think they could see in the sky?
- What is a constellation?
- Why is one of the constellations called the Great Bear?
- What did sailors use the stars to do?
- What is a signpost?

The night sky

Inky, Snake, and Bee were looking up at the night sky. They had found a high spot, away from lights, so the stars were bright.

Earlier, Phonic had explained to them that people long ago thought they could see shapes and pictures in the stars.

"Sets of stars are called constellations," Phonic said, and showed them a picture of the Great Bear on his screen. "See if you can spot this constellation tonight."

"There's the Great Bear!" said Inky, later that night. "Travelers and sailors used to use stars to find their way before there were roads and signposts."

"I'm hoping to see some shooting stars," sighed Bee. "Shooting stars aren't really stars," said Snake. "They're bits of rock falling into Earth's atmosphere and burning up."

"Well, I still like to think of them as shooting stars," replied Bee.

Great Bear constellation

42

Story time

Further reading

Read some stories and books about stars and nighttime, for example:

Children's Picture Atlas of the Stars Tom Kerss (author) and Steve Evans (illustrator)

One Snowy Night Nick Butterworth

Mole's Star Britta Teckentrup

Rhyme time

Encourage the children to repeat this rhyme with you:

*Twinkle, twinkle, little star,
How I wonder what you are.
Up above the sky so high,
Like a diamond in the sky.
Twinkle, twinkle, little star,
How I wonder what you are.*

UNIT 21: Reading comprehension lesson

 3. Comprehension activities

Look at Student Book page 43 with the class. Tell the children to:

1. Read the phrases and draw a picture for each one.
2. Complete the yes / no questions by circling the correct answer.
3. Read and answer the questions. Encourage the children to write in sentences.

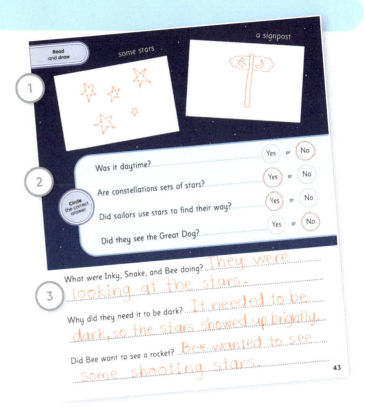

The children can also...
- Find any words in the story with an <igh> spelling.
- Read the passage with a partner.
- Draw a picture and write a sentence from the story.

 4. Plenary

Read the story again as a class. Encourage the children to use the punctuation to help them read with expression and fluency.

 Further activities

- Find out about stars.
- Look at some constellations.
- Draw a pattern in a star shape.

Learning objectives

The children are learning to:
- Listen to, discuss, and recall details from story texts.
- Link what they hear or read to their own experiences.
- Discuss word meanings, linking new words to those they already know.
- Recite rhymes by heart.

Me, myself, and I

UNIT 21: Writing skills lesson

 1. Introductory activity

Remind the children of the writing they did in the last lesson about their favorite story character. Ask the children which character they wrote about, then choose some of the character sketches to look at and read out to the class.

 2. Talk about the writing

Tell the class that Inky, Snake, Bee, and Phonic are friends. The friends like doing things together. Ask what they were doing in the Night Sky story and if any of the children have looked at the stars in the night sky. Ask the children to think about themselves and their friends. Which adjectives would they use to describe themselves? Choose some children and ask them for words that describe themselves, for example: tall, blonde, brown-eyed, happy, strong, good, naughty, kind, and helpful. Ask the children what their favorite color is, what they like doing, who their friends are, and whether they have any hobbies they share with their friends.

 3. Writing activity

1. Tell the children to think of some adjectives to describe themselves and to write them down.
2. Ask the children to think of what they do and what they like doing and to write some of these down. Explain that these are just notes to help them do some writing, so they do not need to write in sentences.
3. The children then use these notes and ideas to write about themselves. Remind them that for this part of the writing they **do** need to write in sentences.

The children can also...

Re-read their work, ensuring it makes sense.

Draw a picture of themselves to go with the writing.

 4. Plenary

Share some of the children's work, either by showing it to the other children or by asking some of them to read out what they have written. The teacher could read out some of the descriptions, and the children can try to identify the who wrote it.

98

UNIT 21: Writing skills lesson

Further activities

- Paint some self portraits.
- Look at famous self-portraits, for example: Vincent Van Gogh, Pablo Picasso, Frida Kahlo, Leonardo da Vinci, Yayoi Kusama, and Lois Mailou Jones.
- Encourage the children to talk to a friend and find out what they like doing. See if they can find out something they didn't know about them. The children could do a piece of writing about their friend, like the one they did about themselves.

Assessment

 The child thinks of some words to describe themself and writes some sentences using plausible spellings and some punctuation; gives adjectives and descriptions mostly about themself.

 The child thinks of some words to describe themself and writes some sentences independently, with correct spellings for most known and regular words; makes plausible attempts at spelling unknown and irregular words; gives adjectives and descriptions mostly about themself.

 The child thinks of some words to describe themself and writes some sentences independently, with correct spellings for most known and regular words; makes plausible attempts at spelling unknown and irregular words; gives adjectives and descriptions, including non-physical characteristics, mostly about themself.

Learning objectives

The children are learning to:
- Discuss what they are going to write about and say a sentence using adjectives.
- Understand some grammatical terminology (adjective).
- Write notes and simple sentences.
- Write words using phonically plausible spellings.
- Re-read their writing to check that it makes sense.

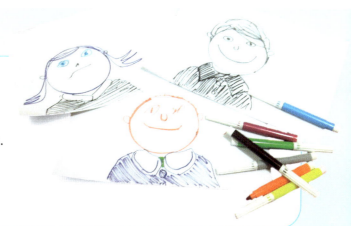

Monster party

UNIT 22: Reading comprehension lesson

📖 1. Read the story

Read the story to the class. Ensure the children can see the text, pointing to the words as you read. Read the story again, sounding out any difficult or unusual words, such as *shy, shiny, skylark, stumbles,* and *straight*. Check that the children know the meaning of these words. Briefly look at the punctuation and point out the speech marks, as well as the exclamation points.

💬 2. Talk about the story

- Where does the monster live?
- What does the monster look like?
- Why is the monster happy?
- Why does she start to jog?
- What does the monster hear?
- Why does she stumble?
- What adjectives are in the story to describe the monster?
- Why does the monster think she looks perfect for a monster party?

Monster party

Out of a dark cave steps a shy monster, with a hairy, green body, webbed toes, and two beady, bright eyes. In her hand she holds a gift tied with a shiny ribbon.

The monster smiles, showing pointed, white teeth. She is happy because she is going to her friend's birthday party. She walks along the path under the tall trees and, because she is a bit late, she starts to jog.

She hears a skylark singing and looks up to try to see the bird. As she does, she trips over a tree root and stumbles straight into a muddy pond!

She sits up. Now she is a muddy, soggy, smelly, green monster.

"No need to go home and get dry," she cries. "I look perfect for a monster party!"

44

Story time

Further reading

Read some stories and books about monsters, for example:

Billy and the Mini Monsters series Zanna Davidson (author) and Melanie Williamson (illustrator)

We're Going to Find the Monster! Malorie Blackman (author) and Dapo Adeola (illustrator)

Fungus the Bogeyman Raymond Briggs

The World's Worst Monsters David Walliams (author) and Adam Stower (illustrator)

Rhyme time

Encourage the children to repeat this rhyme with you:

> Monster, monster, turn around.
> Monster, monster, touch the ground.
> Monster, monster, wave your paws.
> Monster, monster, show your claws.
> Monster, monster, growl and roar,
> Grrrrrrrrrrrrrrrrrrr!

UNIT 22: Reading comprehension lesson

3. Comprehension activities

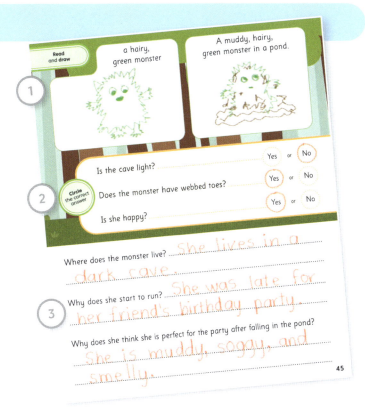

Look at Student Book page 45 with the class. Tell the children to:

1. Read the phrases and draw a picture for each one.
2. Complete the yes / no questions by circling the correct answer.
3. Read and answer the questions. Encourage the children to write in sentences.

The children can also...
- Find all the words in the story with a <y> spelling, saying /ie/.
- Read the passage with a partner.
- Draw a picture of a monster party.

4. Plenary

Read the story again as a class. Encourage the children to read with expression and fluency.

Further activities

- Paint a picture of the monster.
- Describe one of the monsters from one of the Jolly Readers. Can the class or group guess which monster it is? Can they draw the monster?
- Think of adjectives that might describe monsters. Write them around pictures of monsters.

Learning objectives

The children are learning to:
- Listen to, discuss, and recall details from story texts.
- Discuss word meanings, linking new words to those they already know.
- Understand grammatical terminology (adjective).
- Recite rhymes by heart.

UNIT 22: Writing skills lesson

Monsters

Before class

Find some books about monsters, such as the **Monster Party** (Jolly Phonics Reader, Yellow Level, General Fiction). If the class requires an e-book of this title, one can be downloaded from https://jollylearning.com/ereader-aep

1. Introductory activity

Remind the children that adjectives are words that describe nouns. Look at some of the different monsters in books. Point to a few of the monsters and ask the children for adjectives to describe the creatures. Write some of these adjectives on the board.

2. Talk about the writing

Tell the children that they are going to start this piece of work by thinking up their own monster. Ask some questions and suggest ideas as to how their monster might look. Ask the children to think what shape the monster's body and head are, for example.

- Does the monster have a head and a neck?
- Does the monster stand upright or on four (or more) feet?
- Is the creature huge or tiny?
- How many eyes does the monster have? Where are the eyes? What color are they?
- How many ears does the monster have? Where are the ears? Are they big or little?
- Does the monster have legs? Are they long or short? Do they have claws?
- Is the mouth big or small? Does it have teeth or fangs?
- Is the monster furry or smooth? What colors or patterns does the skin or fur have?
- Does the monster have a tail? Is it long or short?

3. Writing activity

1. Tell the children to draw a picture of their monster. (Give them a time limit for the drawing.)

2. Ask the children to write some adjectives to describe their monster around their drawing. (For example: *big, green, hairy, friendly, short, one-eyed, fierce*.) Make sure that the class considers non-physical, as well as physical, characteristics.

3. Tell the children to think about their monster's life: Where does it live? (*In a cave, up a mountain, in a forest, under the stairs, in a pond, in a secret room, in a castle*). Does the monster have a family or friends? Is the monster scary? If so, the children can think about who or what the monster scares and why.

4. Tell the children to think about the name of their monster. Explain that the name might be a made-up word, for example *Zom*—in which case, the child sounds the word out to decide how to spell the name. The children can write the monster's name on their drawing.

5. The children write about their monster.

> **The children can also...**
> Finish drawing and coloring their monster.
> Show, and describe, their monster to a partner.

102

UNIT 22: Writing skills lesson

 4. Plenary

Share some of the children's work, either by showing it to the other children or by asking some of them to read the descriptions of their monster.

 Further activities

- Write next to their picture what noise their monster makes or what it says, then draw a speech bubble around the writing.
- Make a collage of their monster.
- Make a display of the monster collages and their monster noises.

 Assessment

The child writes a few words, most of which are plausibly spelled, but with little or no punctuation.

The child writes a basic description of their monster, mostly about the physical characteristics; uses plausible spellings and some periods.

The child writes a description of their monster, with added details about them as well as the physical characteristics; writes independently in sentences and uses periods and correct spellings of most known and regular words; makes plausible attempts at spelling irregular and unknown words.

Learning objectives

The children are learning to:
- Discuss what they are going to write about.
- Understand and use grammatical terminology (adjective).
- Write simple descriptive sentences.
- Write words using phonically plausible spellings.
- Re-read their writing to check that it makes sense.

The abominable snowman

UNIT 23: Reading comprehension lesson

 1. Read the story

Read the story to the class. Ensure the children can see the text, pointing to the words as you read. Read the story again, sounding out any difficult or unusual words, such as *abominable*, *huge*, *swirled*, and *squinted*. Check that the children know the meaning of these words. Briefly look at the punctuation and mention the speech marks, exclamation points, and question marks.

The abominable snowman

It had been snowing, so Inky, Snake, and Bee were building a snowman.

"I don't want to make just any snowman. I want to make our own abominable snowman!" Snake cried.

They piled up snow until they had a huge mound. Then, they made a head and used two yellow tennis balls for eyes. They gave the snowman long arms with elbows and big feet.

"He really does look abominable," squeaked Inky.

That night before going to bed, Inky looked out of the window. In the dark, the snowflakes swirled around, making it difficult to see. She squinted. Where was their abominable snowman?

She quickly put on her coat and boots and went outside. Big, snowy footprints led away, across the garden and into the darkness. Their abominable snowman had gone!

46

 2. Talk about the story

- What were Inky, Snake, and Bee doing?
- What did Snake want to make?
- What does *abominable* mean?
- What is an abominable snowman?
- What did Inky, Snake, and Bee use for eyes?
- Why was it difficult for Inky to see out of the window later?
- What did Inky see when she went outside?
- Where do you think the abominable snowman went?

Story time

Further reading

Read some stories and books about abominable snowmen, for example:

The Abominable Snowman Terry Pratchett

The Abominables Eva Ibbotson (author) and Jamie Littler and Sharon Rentta (illustrators)

Horrid Henry and the Abominable Snowman Francesca Simon (author) and Tony Ross (illustrator)

The Abominable Snow Baby Daniel Fanelli (author) and Jenna Bertino (illustrator)

Rhyme time

Encourage the children to repeat this rhyme with you:

Round and round the village,
The abominable footprints go
Hopping, skipping,
Then vanish with the snow.

UNIT 23: Reading comprehension lesson

3. Comprehension activities

Look at Student Book page 47 with the class. Tell the children to:

1. Read the phrase and draw a picture.
2. Complete the yes / no questions by circling the correct answer.
3. Read and answer the questions. Encourage the children to write in sentences.

> **The children can also…**
>
> Find all the words with an <ow> spelling, saying /oa/.
>
> Read the story with a partner.
>
> With a partner, talk about where they think the abominable snowman went and what he did.

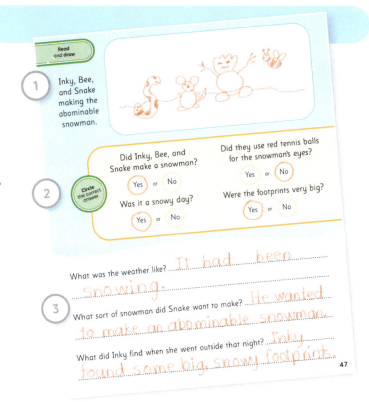

4. Plenary

Read the story again as a class. Encourage the children to use the punctuation to help them read with expression and fluency. Ask the children what they think might have happened to the abominable snowman: where did he go and what did he do?

Further activities

- Watch Terry Pratchett's film **The Abominable Snow Baby**.
- Draw, or paint, snowy pictures.
- Draw, or paint, an abominable snowman or snowmen.

Learning objectives

The children are learning to:
- Listen to, discuss, and recall details from different types of texts.
- Discuss word meanings, linking new words to those they already know.
- Use and explain prediction, adding more detail.
- Recite rhymes by heart.

UNIT 23: Writing skills lesson

The abominable snowman

 ## 1. Introductory activity

Remind the children about the story of **The abominable snowman**. Explain that abominable snowmen are mythical creatures and no one has ever seen one. There have been lots of stories about giant creatures, sometimes called yetis, which are thought to live high up in the Himalayan mountains. People claim to have seen their footprints, but no one can prove that yetis or abominable snowmen exist. Ask the children to think of other imaginary creatures, such as:

- **The Gruffalo** by Julia Donaldson (author) and Axel Scheffler (illustrator)
- **Where the Wild Things Are** by Maurice Sendak
- **Shrek**, the DreamWorks film series
- **Monsters Inc.**, the Disney–Pixar film

The abominable snowman

It had been snowing, so Inky, Snake, and Bee were building a snowman.

"I don't want to make just any snowman. I want to make our own abominable snowman!" Snake cried.

They piled up snow until they had a huge mound. Then, they made a head and used two yellow tennis balls for eyes. They gave the snowman long arms with elbows and big feet.

"He really does look abominable," squeaked Inky.

That night before going to bed, Inky looked out of the window. In the dark, the snowflakes swirled around, making it difficult to see. She squinted. Where was their abominable snowman?

She quickly put on her coat and boots and went outside. Big, snowy footprints led away, across the garden and into the darkness. Their abominable snowman had gone!

46

 ## 2. Talk about the writing

Look at some of the monsters the children have drawn and described during the previous reading comprehension lesson in unit 22. Choose some children to say a few sentences about their monster.

 ## 3. Writing activity

1. Tell the children to imagine that one night their monster meets an abominable snowman. Encourage the class to think about where the monsters meet and whether the abominable snowman is happy, scared, or frightened. The children consider whether the two creatures make friends, where they go and what they might do.
2. The children write about their monster meeting the abominable snowman.

The children can also...

- Draw a picture to illustrate their writing.
- Discuss whether there is any folklore from their part of the world about yeti-like creatures.
- Re-read their work, ensuring it makes sense.

106

UNIT 23: Writing skills lesson

 4. Plenary

Share some of the children's work, either by showing it to the other children or by asking some of them to read out what they have written.

 Further activities

- Look at footprints made by different animals.
- Draw or cut out some different shaped and sized footprints and ask the children to imagine what or who made them. Then, the children can draw a picture to illustrate what made the prints.
- Design shoes for an abominable snowman or snow woman.
- Make paper snowflakes.

 Assessment

The child writes a few sentences about the two monsters meeting; uses some periods and capital letters; makes plausible attempts at spelling most known and regular words.

The child writes in sentences independently, about the two monsters meeting; adds details and ideas of their own; uses correct spellings of most known and regular words; makes plausible attempts at spelling unknown and irregular words.

The child writes several sentences independently, about the two monsters meeting; uses correct or plausible spellings of most known and regular words.

Learning objectives

The children are learning to:
- Discuss what they are going to write about.
- Understand different types of story (folklore).
- Write simple sentences to create a sequence of events (narrative).
- Write words using phonically plausible spellings.
- Re-read their writing to check that it makes sense.

107

UNIT 24: Reading comprehension lesson

Monster Times

 1. Read the report

Read the story to the class. Ensure the children can see the text, pointing to the words as you read. Read the story again, sounding out any difficult or unusual words, such as *reporter, enormous, police, bounding, gigantic, sighting,* and *mystery*. Check that the children know the meaning of these words. Point out that *snowman, footprints,* and *newspaper* are compound words.

> **Explain that...**
>
> ...the story is a made-up (fictional) report for a newspaper, the **Monster Times**. Talk briefly about newspapers and why people read them. Stories in newspapers begin with a short headline which tells you, in a few words, the main point of the story.

Monster Times

Abominable Sight
Reporter: Jim Chew

There have been reports of a massive abominable snowman in the local area. Sets of enormous footprints have been found in the snow.

"When I went out last night I could see huge footprints across my garden," said Inky Mouse.

Police were also called to Hillside Farm yesterday after reports that a giant, hairy, white creature had been seen bounding across the fields. A track of gigantic footprints could be clearly seen in the snow. The footprints led to the Vowel Forest, but then disappeared.

Footprints have been found in a few places, but there has only been one sighting of the abominable snowman.

"It is a mystery," said Officer Jewel from the local police.

48

 2. Talk about the report

- What does a reporter do?
- What had people been reporting?
- Why did the police go to Hillside Farm?
- What had the creature been seen doing?
- How did people know something had really been there?
- Where did the footprints lead?
- What words in the story mean *big*?
- Why do you think the abominable snowman went into the Vowel Forest?

Story time

Further reading

Read some stories and books about newspapers and reporters, for example:

Horrid Henry's Newspaper
Francesca Simon (author) and
Tony Ross (illustrator)

The Newspaper Kids series Juanita Phillips

Geronimo Stilton Reporter series
Elisabetta Dami (author)

How the News Works Jane Marlow (author) and Terri Po (illustrator)

Rhyme time

Encourage the children to sing this rhyme with you (to the tune of **Frère Jacques**):

> *Abominable snowman, abominable snowman,*
> *Where are you? Where are you?*
> *Running through the sn-ow, running through the sn-ow.*
> *Can't catch me! Can't catch me!*

UNIT 24: Reading comprehension lesson

3. Comprehension activities

Look at Student Book page 49 with the class. Tell the children to:

1. Read the phrase and draw a picture.
2. Complete the yes / no questions by circling the correct answer.
3. Read and answer the questions. Encourage the children to write in complete sentences.
4. Write down four words from the text that also mean *big*.

> **The children can also...**
> - Find all the words with an <ew> spelling, saying /ue/.
> - Find any compound words in the report.
> - Read the story with a partner.

4. Plenary

Read the story again as a class. Encourage the children to use the punctuation to help them read with expression and fluency.

Further activities

- Draw a picture from the story.
- Make prints with their own hands and feet.
- Compare foot sizes.
- Make footprints with a sponge or potato that has been cut to look like a foot.

Learning objectives

The children are learning to:
- Listen to, discuss, and recall details from stories and nonfiction.
- Link what they hear or read to their own experiences.
- Discuss the significance of the title and events.
- Discuss word meanings, linking new words to those they already know.
- Use images to support their understanding of the text.
- Use and explain prediction, adding more detail.

UNIT 24: Writing skills lesson

Monster Meeting!

1. Introductory activity

Talk about newspapers. Explain that newspapers are published daily or weekly and contain reports about things that happen. They might be about world events or things happening locally. Look at a children's newspaper or a local newspaper. Point out the newspaper's name, or title. Next, point to a headline, which is a short sentence or phrase about the news story. Newspapers also have the date printed on each sheet.

2. Talk about the writing

Tell the children they are going to write a report about the two monsters meeting. Suggest that the headline for this meeting could be **Monster Meeting!** Talk about why the headline has an exclamation point. Explain that the exclamation point can refer to the excitement of two monsters meeting. The point can also refer to using the word *monster* to mean *huge*, implying something big, or important, has happened. The headline is written in big letters.

Newspaper reports tend to be fairly short and retell only the known facts about a story. The reports might say that the monster is large or a certain color, but do not describe the creatures in lots of detail.

Explain that...

...newspaper articles are usually written in columns that do not cross the whole page.

(Many newspapers were originally printed on broad sheets of paper across which lines of long text would be hard to read.)

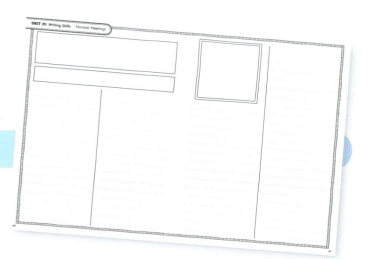

3. Writing activity

1. Tell the children to copy the newspaper name (**Monster Times**) and the headline, **Monster Meeting!** Remind the children to use big letters for the headline.

2. Ask the children to write a report about the two monsters meeting, including information such as where the meeting was held, who saw the meeting, and what the monsters did and said at the meeting. If the students are writing on paper, tell the children to fold the sheet in half vertically and write down one side and then down the other side, so their report is in columns.

The children can also...

- Draw a picture to illustrate the report.
- Re-read their work, ensuring it makes sense.
- Read their work to a partner.

UNIT 24: Writing skills lesson

4. Plenary

Share some of the children's work, either by showing it to the other children or by asking some of them to read out what they have written.

Further activities

- Look at some real newspapers.
- Cut letters out from newspaper headlines to make words or pictures.
- Make a collage from shapes and pictures cut out from a newspaper.

Assessment

The child writes some words or sentences about the monsters meeting using plausible spellings, but little or no punctuation.

The child writes independently about the monsters meeting, mostly using ideas from the story, uses plausible spellings and some periods and capital letters.

The child writes independently about the monsters meeting, making up details about what has taken place; uses correct spellings for most known and regular words; makes plausible attempts at spelling unknown and irregular words and uses periods and capital letters.

Learning objectives

The children are learning to:
- Discuss what they are going to write about.
- Understand different types of writing (newspaper reports).
- Write simple sentences to create a sequence of events (narrative).
- Write words using phonically plausible spellings.
- Re-read their writing to check that it makes sense.

UNIT 25: Reading comprehension lesson

Cloud watching

 1. Read the story

Read the story to the class. Ensure the children can see the text, pointing to the words as you read. Read the story again, sounding out any difficult or unusual words, such as *blown, whale, curving, abominable,* and *chuckled.* Check that the children know the meaning of these words.

 2. Talk about the story

- Where were Inky, Snake, and Bee?
- What were they doing?
- Why is a hill a good place to watch clouds?
- What was making the clouds move?
- What things did they think the clouds looked like?
- What did Bee notice?
- What did Bee suggest they should do?
- Discuss whether the children in the class have ever looked for shapes in the clouds.

Cloud watching

Inky, Bee, and Snake were outside, sitting on the top of a hill. They were looking up at the big, fluffy clouds being blown along by the wind.

"That cloud looks like a house with windows," said Inky.

"And that one looks like a whale with a big, open mouth, swimming along in the sky," added Bee.

"Those clouds are all coming together to look like a dragon. There's the head, and those smaller, round clouds make a curving body and long tail," said Snake.

"And that one over there looks like a big cloud footprint. Even bigger than the abominable snowman's," he chuckled.

"I don't want to worry anyone, but look at those huge, gray clouds gathering in the distance!" said Bee. "I think perhaps it is time we headed home before we get wet."

50

Story time

Further reading

Read some stories and books about clouds, for example:

Cloud Babies Eoin Colfer (author) and Chris Judge (illustrator)

Cloud Tea Monkeys Mal Peet and Elspeth Graham (authors) and Juan Wijngaard (illustrator)

Cyril the Lonely Cloud Tim Hopgood

Clouds and Fog Jolly Phonics Reader, Blue Level, Our World

Rhyme time

Recite the rhyme with the class.

> *White sheep, white sheep,*
> *On a blue hill,*
> *When the wind stops*
> *You all stand still.*
> *When the wind blows*
> *You walk away slow.*
> *White sheep, white sheep,*
> *Where do you go?*
>
> By Christina Rossetti

112

UNIT 25: Reading comprehension lesson

3. Comprehension activities

Look at Student Book page 51 with the class. Tell the children to:

1. Complete the yes / no questions by circling the correct answer.
2. Read and answer the questions. Encourage the children to write in sentences.

The children can also...
- Find all the words in the story with an <ou> spelling, saying /ou/.
- Read the story with a partner.
- Draw a picture and write a sentence from the story.

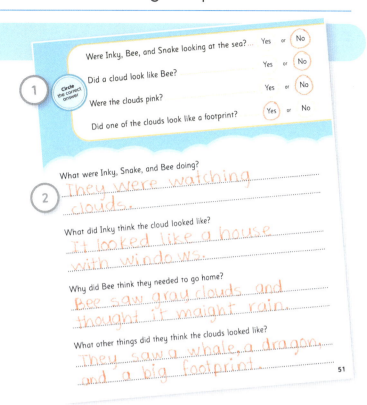

4. Plenary

Read the story again as a class. Encourage the children to use the punctuation to help them read with expression and fluency.

Further activities

- Go cloud watching.
- Paint a picture of different types of clouds.
- Look at paintings that include clouds.

Learning objectives

The children are learning to:
- Listen to, discuss, and recall details from stories.
- Link what they hear or read to their own experiences.
- Discuss word meanings, linking new words to those they already know.
- Use inference and prediction.

113

UNIT 25: Writing skills lesson

Cloud watching

 1. Introductory activity

If possible, go cloud watching. Encourage the children to think about what they see and hear, and how they feel.

 2. Talk about the writing

Discuss clouds and how their shapes change in different weathers. Find, or take, some pictures of clouds. Ask the children to draw on them and see if they can turn them into pictures of other things.

 3. Writing activity

1. Tell the children to write about what they saw, heard, and felt when they were watching the clouds. The writing can be done in a cloud shape.

2. Then, tell the class they are going to write an acrostic poem about clouds. In an acrostic poem, each line starts with a letter from the word:

   Clouds blowing across the sky
   Look like an
   Octopus with waving arms
   Up in the sky, cats
   Dancing and twirling
   Storm clouds chasing everything away.

   Clouds
   Like white fluffy pillows
   On their travels
   Up so high
   Dashing about
   Shadows passing over me.

The children can write their poem in a cloud shape, with the letters at the beginning of each line in a color (as above).

The children can also...
- Re-read their work, ensuring it makes sense.
- Decorate their writing by drawing illustrations for their poems.

 4. Plenary

Share some of the children's work, either by showing it to the other children or by asking some of them to read out what they have written.

114

UNIT 25: Writing skills lesson

 Further activities

- Find out about the different types of clouds and their names.
- Outline some cloud shapes and doodle faces on them or turn them into animals.
- Cut out cloud shapes together and write on dreams, hopes, and wishes on them.

 Assessment

The child writes some sentences with correct spellings of regular and known words; suggests or writes a word beginning with the right letter; makes plausible attempts at spelling irregular and unknown words; may need support to see shapes or images of other things in clouds.

The child says how they feel or writes independently in sentences about how they feel with correct spellings of regular and known words; makes plausible attempts at spelling irregular and unknown words; suggests or writes a phrase or sentence beginning with the right letter; sees shapes or images in clouds, and imagines what some clouds could be.

The child says how they feel or writes independently in sentences about how they feel with correct spellings of regular and known words; makes plausible attempts at spelling irregular and unknown words; suggests or writes a word or phrase beginning with the right letter; sees shapes or images in clouds.

Learning objectives

The children are learning to:
- Discuss what they are going to write about.
- Understand different types of writing.
- Use a simple plan (acrostic poem) to support or organize writing.
- Say a sentence.
- Write simple sentences.
- Write words using phonically plausible spellings.

115

UNIT 26: Reading comprehension lesson

Monster verbs

 1. Read the rhyme

Read the rhyme to the class. Ensure the children can see the text, pointing to the words as you read. Read the rhyme again, sounding out any difficult or unusual words, such as *flown, preen,* and *swamp.* Check that the children know the meaning of these words. Point out that in order to rhyme, words have to sound the same, but are not necessarily spelled the same.

 2. Talk about the rhyme

- What is a verb?
- What is a rhyme?
- What does *flown* mean?
- Why would monsters gleam?
- What do monsters do in a swamp?
- Where do monsters fly and cry?
- What does *prowl* mean?

Story time

Further reading

Read some stories and books that rhyme, for example:

The Usborne Rhyming Alphabet
Felicity Brooks (author) and Gareth Lucas (illustrator)

Ten Delicious Teachers
Ross Montgomery (author) and Sarah Warburton (illustrator)

Dr. Seuss series
Dr. Seuss / Theodor Geisel (author)

The Troll Julia Donaldson (author) and David Roberts (illustrator)

Rhyme time

For this activity, all the class say the first two lines together, then a child is chosen to pick a verb. They say the next two lines and act out the verb. The rest of the class then repeat the words and do the action. The rhyme is then repeated with a different child choosing the verb each time.

All: *One little monster came out to play,*
What is it that we're doing today?

Child: *Today we're all flapping, flapping, flapping.*
Today we're all flapping, flapping, flapping.

All: *Today we're all flapping, flapping, flapping.*
Today we're all flapping, flapping, flapping.

All: *Another little monster came out to play,*
What is it that we're doing today?

UNIT 26: Reading comprehension lesson

3. Comprehension activities

Look at Student Book page 53 with the class. Tell the children to:

1. Complete the yes / no questions by circling the correct answer.
2. Read and answer the questions. Encourage the children to write in sentences.

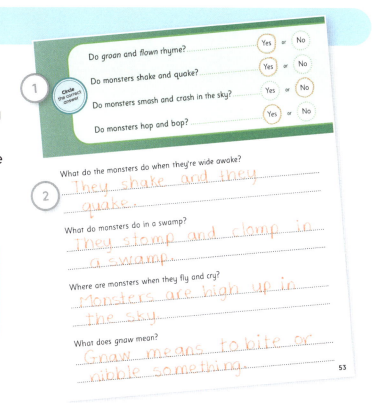

> **The children can also...**
> - Read the rhyme with a partner.
> - Underline the words that rhyme in each verse.
> - Draw a picture from the rhyme.

4. Plenary

Read the rhyme again as a class. Ask some children how they answered the questions.

Further activities

- Use the blends wheel to find words that rhyme.
- Work with a partner to think up more verses for the rhyme.
- Draw pictures illustrating the new verses.

Learning objectives

The children are learning to:
- Listen to, discuss, and recall details from poems and rhymes.
- Understand grammatical terminology (verb).
- Discuss word meanings, linking new words to those they already know.
- Recite rhymes and poems (some by heart).

117

UNIT 26: Writing skills lesson

Monster verbs

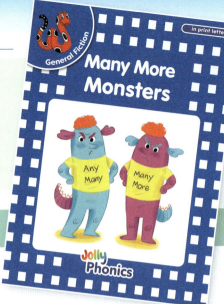

Before class
Make sure the class has access to the **Many More Monsters** (Jolly Phonics Reader, Blue Level, General Fiction). If the class requires an e-book of this title, one can be downloaded from https://jollylearning.com/ereader-aep

 1. Introductory activity

With the class, read the story **I saw a monster** from **Many More Monsters**. Look at the rhyming words with the children. Point out that it is the sound of the rhyming word that is important and not the word's spelling. Some sounds can be spelled in different ways; for example, <ai> <ay> <a-e> all make an /ai/ sound.

 2. Talk about the writing

Write some words on the board or on small cards. Pick a word and ask the children to think of, or choose, other words that rhyme with that word. As a class or in groups, the children then sort the words into rhyming sets. Some examples of rhyming words are:

- *owl, howl, yowl, prowl, foul*
- *flower, power, shower, cower*
- *round, sound, found, hound, mound*
- *out, shout, pout, spout, sprout*
- *best, nest, pest, rest, west*
- *hush, rush, brush, crush*
- *sweet, treat, beat, seat, fleet, tweet, street*
- *light, night, fright, kite*
- *boat, float, wrote, gloat, throat, note*

 3. Writing activity

1. Tell the children to choose a word, then find or think of another word that rhymes with their choice.
2. Then, ask the children to think of a sentence, using the two rhyming words. For example:

   Monster in a shower, smells like a flower!

   Monsters build a nest, then they have a rest.
3. Encourage the children to write as many sentences as they can.

The children can also...
- Choose their favorite sentences, write them neatly on another sheet of paper and draw pictures to illustrate the words.
- Make a class display or book of these rhymes.
- Find and read books with rhymes in.

UNIT 26: Writing skills lesson

 4. Plenary

Share some of the children's work, either by showing it to the other children or by asking some of them to read out their favorite pair of rhyming sentences.

 Further activities

- Find books about monsters and make a display.
- Draw, paint, or collage monsters.
- Make a collection of verbs.
- Play *Inky (or Simon) says*. Say a verb and the children do an action for the verb, but only if it is preceded by *Inky says…*

 Assessment

The child identifies rhyming words and attempts to write two rhyming sentences with plausible spellings of most regular and known words; attempts to use punctuation.

The child identifies rhyming words and writes independently two rhyming sentences with correct spellings of most regular and known words; makes plausible attempts to spell irregular and unknown words; nearly always uses punctuation correctly.

The child identifies or thinks of their own rhyming words and writes independently two rhyming sentences with correct spellings of most regular and known words; makes plausible attempts to spell irregular and unknown words; nearly always uses punctuation correctly.

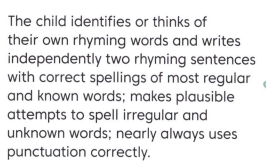

Learning objectives

The children are learning to:
- Discuss what they are going to write about.
- Understand different types of text (poetry and rhymes).
- Understand grammatical terminology (verb).
- Use a simple plan (rhyming) to support or organize writing.
- Say a sentence.
- Write simple sentences.
- Write words using phonically plausible spellings.

119

UNIT 27: Reading comprehension lesson

The chatty tortoise

Before class

Make sure the class has access to **The Chatty Tortoise** (Jolly Phonics Folktales, Green Level). If the class requires an e-book of this title, one can be downloaded from
https://jollylearning.com/ereader-aep

1. Read the fable

Read the story to the class. Ensure the children can see the text, pointing to the words as you read. Read the story again, sounding out any difficult or unusual words, such as *tortoise*, *chatted*, *exclaimed*, and *laughed*. Check that the children know the meaning of these words. Briefly look at the punctuation and mention the speech marks and the exclamation points.

2. Talk about the fable

- Where did the tortoise live?
- What did he like doing?
- Why were the geese leaving?
- Why would it be difficult for the tortoise to go to the other lake?
- How were the geese going to take him?
- What happened when the tortoise started to talk?
- Why is the word *fell* written as it is?
- Why did the tortoise never talk again?

Story time

Further reading

Read some stories and books about tortoises, for example:

The Elephant's Friend and Other Tales from Ancient India retold by Marcia Williams

Albert in the Air Ian Brown (author) and Eoin Clarke (illustrator)

The Hare and the Tortoise retold by Helen Ward

George the Grumpy Tortoise Catherine Bensley

Rhyme time

Encourage the class to learn this poem with you and recite it together:

Tortoise, tortoise, where are you?
Hiding in your shell.
Tortoise, tortoise, what do you do
When I can't see you?

120

UNIT 27: Reading comprehension lesson

3. Comprehension activities

Look at Student Book page 55 with the class. Tell the children to:

1. Complete the yes / no questions by circling the correct answer.

2. Read and answer the questions. Encourage the children to write in sentences.

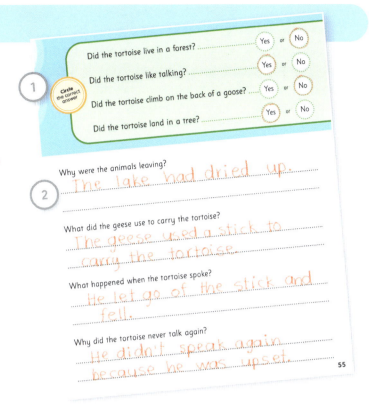

The children can also...

- Find all the words in the story with an /oi/ sound.
- Underline any adverbs in the story in orange.
- Read the story with a partner.

 ## 4. Plenary

Read the story again as a class. Encourage the children to use the punctuation to help them read with expression and fluency.

 ## Further activities

- Find out about tortoises.
- Paint a picture of a tortoise.
- Ask the class to try and keep quiet for as long as possible, just like the tortoise did at the end of the story. Can the children last a whole minute?

Learning objectives

The children are learning to:
- Listen to, discuss, and recall details from story texts.
- Become familiar with, and retell, traditional stories and rhymes.
- Discuss word meanings, linking new words to those they already know.
- Use inferences.

The chatty tortoise

UNIT 27: Writing skills lesson

The chatty tortoise

Before class
Make sure the class has access to the **The Chatty Tortoise** (Jolly Phonics Folktales, Green Level). If the class requires an e-book of this title, one can be downloaded from https://jollylearning.com/ereader-aep

 1. Introductory activity

Remind the children about the Jolly Phonics Folktales, **The Chatty Tortoise**. As a class, read the shorter version of **The Chatty Tortoise** in the Student Book again.

 2. Talk about the writing

Discuss the story with the class. If possible, look at the pictures from the Jolly Phonics Folktales version. Talk about the story and ask the children lots of questions about what happened, for example:

- What did the tortoise like doing? Where did he live and who did he talk to?
- How did the tortoise feel when all the other animals and birds were going away?
- What did the tortoise think?
- How did the geese decide they could carry the tortoise?
- What was it like up in the air? What could the tortoise see? Had he ever seen the world from up high before?
- What happened when the tortoise opened his mouth?
- What did it feel like when the tortoise fell?
- What was the tortoise determined to do after the first fall?
- What did the tortoise feel like when the animals laughed? Why did he open his mouth?
- Where did the tortoise land?
- How did the tortoise get down from the tree?

 3. Writing activity

1. Ask the children for some suggestions for a sentence to begin the story.
2. Choose one sentence and model it on the board.
3. Either the children copy the sentence from the board, or they write their own first sentence.
4. Then, ask the children to continue the story by writing in sentences and retelling the story of **The Chatty Tortoise**.

The children can also...
- Re-read their work, ensuring it makes sense.
- Draw a picture to illustrate the story.

UNIT 27: Writing skills lesson

 4. Plenary

Share some of the children's work, either by showing it to the other children or by asking some of them to read out what they have written.

 Further activities

- Try to talk for a minute, without stopping.
- Learn some Makaton or American Sign Language.
- Find out how to say *hello* and *thank you* in other languages.

 Assessment

 The child writes some sentences, retelling some of the story with plausible spellings of most words, but little punctuation.

 The child writes some sentences independently, covering at least a page and retelling the basic story; uses some ideas from the picture and uses correct or plausible spellings for known and regular words; makes plausible attempts at spelling irregular and unknown words.

 The child writes one or two pages independently, mostly in sentences with periods and correct spellings of most known or regular words; makes plausible attempts at spelling irregular and unknown words; uses some ideas from the pictures and knowledge from the story, as well as adding extra information.

Learning objectives

The children are learning to:
- Discuss what they are going to write about.
- Say a sentence.
- Write simple sentences in a sequence to tell a short story.
- Write words using phonically plausible spellings.
- Re-read their writing to check that it makes sense.

My best toy

UNIT 28: Reading comprehension lesson

 ### 1. Read the story

Read the story to the class. Ensure the children can see the text, pointing to the words as you read. Read the story again, sounding out any difficult or unusual words, such as *announced, people, proudly,* and *annoying.* Check that the children know the meaning of these words. Briefly look at the punctuation and mention the speech marks.

 ### 2. Talk about the story

- What are the children talking about?
- What is Mabel?
- What does Seth like doing?
- What model has he brought?
- Why does Seth say his baby brother is very annoying?
- What is Hamid's favorite toy?
- What does Hamid like to make?
- Do the children in the class have any favorite toys? What are they?

My best toy

"Now," announced Miss Beech to her class. "We have time for three more people to show us their favorite toys."

"My best toy is Mabel," Anna said. "She is a bunny and I was given her when I was two. She sleeps with me every night. My grandma knitted her a sweater and she has some other clothes as well."

Seth carefully took a model of a spaceship out of a box. "I like building things," he declared proudly. "I got this model as a present. I have to keep it up high because my baby brother can be very annoying. He tries to help but he destroys things instead."

"My best toys are my racing cars and track," said Hamid. "I have lots of cars and I enjoy making different tracks and racing my cars around them."

56

Story time

Further reading

Read some stories and books about toys, for example:

The Magical Toy Box Melanie Joyce (author) and James Newman Gray (illustrator)

Toys in Space Mini Grey

Lost in the Toy Museum David Lucas

The Nutcracker E. T. A. Hoffmann

Kipper's Toybox Mick Inkpen

Rhyme time

Encourage the class to recite this rhyme with you:

> Ride a toy horse to Banbury Cross,
> To see a fine lady upon a white horse.
> With rings on her fingers and bells on her toes,
> She shall have music wherever she goes.

UNIT 28: Reading comprehension lesson

 3. Comprehension activities

Look at Student Book page 57 with the class. Tell the children to:

1. Complete the yes / no questions by circling the correct answer.
2. Read and answer the questions. Encourage the children to write in sentences.

The children can also…
- Find all the words with an <oy> spelling, saying /oi/.
- Read the passage with a partner.
- Underline any adverbs with an orange pencil and verbs with a red pencil.

 4. Plenary

Read the story again as a class. Encourage the children to use the punctuation to help them read with expression and fluency.

 Further activities

- Find out about old toys.
- Ask the children to talk about their own favorite toy.
- Ask the children to talk to their parents or grandparents about the favorite toys they had when they were young.

Learning objectives

The children are learning to:
- Listen to, discuss, and recall details from story texts.
- Link what they hear or read to their own experiences.
- Discuss word meanings, linking new words to those they already know.
- Use prediction.

Toys at midnight

UNIT 28: Writing skills lesson

 1. Introductory activity

Ask the children about their favorite toys. Ask them to say briefly, in sentences, why they like their favorite, and what or how they play with that toy.

 2. Talk about the writing

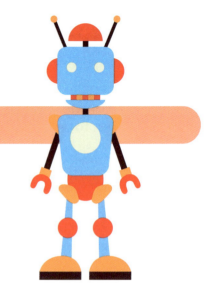

Ask the children what they think their toys at home or in the classroom might get up to at night. Talk about the toys and whether they are kind or friendly, and if any are friends with each other.

- Do the toys like it when their surroundings are quiet? Or do the toys prefer it when it's noisy?
- Do the toys like playing with a particular child?

 3. Writing activity

1. Tell the children to imagine that it is nighttime and the toys have come to life.
2. Ask the class to suggest some opening sentences.
3. Choose some sentences and write them on the board, for example: *It was just past midnight. The room was quiet and everyone was asleep. The lid of the toy box slowly opened and out climbed...*
4. Encourage the children to write about the toys coming to life. Remind them that a story has a beginning, a middle, and an end.

The children can also...
- Re-read their work, ensuring it makes sense.
- Draw a picture to illustrate their story.
- Share their work with a partner.

126

UNIT 28: Writing skills lesson

 4. Plenary

Share some of the children's work, either by showing it to the other children or by asking some of them to read out what they have written.

Further activities

- Watch the Disney–Pixar film, **Toy Story**.
- Design a toy box.
- Play the memory game *In my toy box there is...* One child thinks of a toy. The next child repeats the name of that toy and adds a new toy. The next child says the first toy, the second toy, and adds a third toy. The game continues with the children trying to remember the toys in the correct order.

 Assessment

The child talks about what the toys might do and writes a few words, using plausible spellings, but little punctuation.

The child writes independently at least a page about what the toys might do at night, using some periods and plausible spellings.

The child writes independently in sentences at least one or two pages about what the toys might do at night; uses periods; uses correct spellings of most known and regular words; makes plausible attempts to spell unknown and irregular words.

Learning objectives

The children are learning to:
- Discuss what they are going to write about.
- Say a sentence.
- Write simple sentences to create a sequence of events (narrative).
- Write words using phonically plausible spellings.
- Re-read their writing to check that it makes sense.

UNIT 29: Reading comprehension lesson

Once Upon a Time Street

 1. Read the story

Read the story to the class. Ensure the children can see the text, pointing to the words as you read. Read the story again, sounding out any difficult or unusual words, such as *guess, featherlight, assorted, treasure, pirate, comfy* and *cushion*. Check that the children know the meaning of these words. Point out the proper nouns and explain that they have capital letters.

Once Upon a Time Street

One morning, the delivery van arrived in Once Upon a Time Street. The driver went to deliver the boxes, but found that some of the address labels had rubbed off.

"I'll just have to read what's in the boxes and guess who they are for," he decided. He read the contents on the first box.

"A new wand, some featherlight wing spray, and forty bottles of assorted sparkle-dust. That will be for Fairy Godmother at number four."

"Three treasure maps, a box of telescope-cleaning wipes, and a sack of parrot food. Easy! Pirate Pete at number 40."

"Seashells, a rainbow comb, a songbook, and a comfy cushion. That will be Melody Mermaid at the end of the street."

"All done and sorted," said the driver, smiling as he drove off.

 2. Talk about the story

- What sort of stories begin with *Once upon a time*?
- Why couldn't the driver deliver the boxes?
- What did the driver do?
- Where did Fairy Godmother live?
- Why might Pirate Pete need a sack of parrot food?
- Who lived at number 40?
- What is the mermaid's name?
- Why might she need a comfy cushion?

Story time

Further reading

Read some stories and books about boxes, for example:

The Box Jolly Phonics, Yellow Reader, General Fiction

Boxitects Kim Smith

My Book Box Will Hillenbrand

What to Do with a Box Jane Yolen (author) and Chris Sheban (illustrator)

Rhyme time

This poem can be extended with additional verses as the children suggest varying things that could be in the box (for example, a cat).

What's in the box?
What's in the box?
You don't know and I don't know,
What's in the box?

A cat's in the box,
A cat's in the box,
I know and you know,
A cat's in the box.

UNIT 29: Reading comprehension lesson

3. Comprehension activities

Look at Student Book page 59 with the class. Tell the children to:

1. Complete the yes / no questions by circling the correct answer.
2. Read and answer the questions. Encourage the children to write in sentences.

> **The children can also...**
> - Find all the words in the story with an <or> spelling, saying /or/.
> - Read the story with a partner.
> - Write one of the missing address labels for one of the boxes.

4. Plenary

Read the story again as a class. Encourage the children to use the punctuation to help them read with expression and fluency.

Further activities

- Wrap boxes and write addresses for characters.
- Decorate a special class memory box.
- Collect some big boxes for the children to draw on and play in.

Learning objectives

The children are learning to:
- Listen to, discuss, and recall details from story texts.
- Discuss word meanings, linking new words to those they already know.
- Use images to support their understanding of the text.
- Use inference.
- Appreciate rhymes and poems, and recite some by heart.

Once Upon a Time Street

129

UNIT 29: Writing skills lesson

Character boxes

 1. Introductory activity

Remind the children that characters are people in stories. Remind them about the story of the delivery driver in **Once Upon a Time Street** and ask how he identified which box belonged to which person. Remind them that characters usually have things associated with them that identify the person.

 2. Talk about the writing

Find a box and put some items in the box that would be associated with a particular character. These could be toys, models, or pictures of the items.

For example:

- *Fairy: wand, wings, glitter, picture of a toadstool*
- *Robin Hood: felt hat, toy bow and arrow, some leaves*
- *Anansi: spider's web, pretend flies, book of tricks and jokes*
- *Captain Hook or any pirate: spotty scarf, toy hook, treasure map, cuddly parrot*
- *Princess: crown, sparkly dress, picture of a castle*
- *Puss in boots: hat with a feather, boots, tin of cat food*
- *Chatty tortoise: small stick, toy geese, printed speech bubble*

Take out the items one by one and ask the children to whom that box belongs.

 3. Writing activity

1. Tell the children to think of a character from a story.
2. Then, in a box shape, draw at least three things that might belong to that character and write the name of the character next to the box.
3. Ask the children to write a brief description of their chosen character.
4. Encourage the children to do this for three other characters.

The children can also...

- Draw the character alongside the items.
- Think up and write an address label for each box.

UNIT 29: Writing skills lesson

4. Plenary

Share some of the children's work. Ask some children to say what items are in one of their boxes so the other children can guess which character the items identify.

Further activities

- Draw a map showing where the characters live and add where the boxes were delivered.
- Find out about how parcels are delivered.
- Have other story boxes or bags for the children to use.
- Make a display of books, comics, posters, or pictures of characters from stories.

Assessment

The child thinks of a character from a story and some items to identify that character; attempts to write a description in sentences using correct or plausible spellings.

The child thinks of a character from a story and some items to identify that character; describes that character in their writing as well as mentioning items in the box; writes sentences independently with correct or plausible spellings.

The child thinks of a character from a story and some items to identify that character; describes that character in their writing, mentioning items in the box as well as other details; writes sentences independently with correct spellings for known and regular words; makes plausible attempts at spelling unknown and irregular words.

Learning objectives

The children are learning to:
- Discuss what they are going to write about.
- Discuss the key features of a book (characters).
- Say a sentence.
- Write simple sentences.
- Write words using phonically plausible spellings.
- Re-read their writing to check that it makes sense.

131

UNIT 30: Reading comprehension lesson

Jack and the Beanstalk

 1. Read the story

Read the story to the class. Ensure the children can see the text, pointing to the words as you read. Read the story again, sounding out any difficult or unusual words, such as *cottage*, *magic*, *excitedly*, and *beanstalk*. Check that the children know the meaning of these words.

 2. Talk about the story

- What does *poor* mean?
- Who lived in the cottage?
- What did Jack's mother tell him to do with the cow?
- What did the man give Jack for the cow?
- Why did Jack's mother throw the beans out of the window?
- Why was she cross?
- Why did Jack have to wait until the morning to find the beans?
- What had grown in the garden overnight?
- What do you think Jack will do now?

Jack and the Beanstalk

Jack and his mother lived in a small cottage. They were very poor. Jack's mother told him to take their cow to market to sell her.

After a while, a man walked by and started talking to Jack. "I will give you five magic beans for your cow," he said. "The beans will make you rich for the rest of your life."

Jack ran home and excitedly told his mother about the beans. "You silly boy!" she cried. "Five beans won't make us rich." She threw the beans out of the window.

Jack was cross with his mother but as it was nighttime, he would have to wait to find the beans. But when Jack went out the next morning there was a beanstalk growing up and up and into the clouds.

60

Story time

Further reading

Read other versions of the **Jack and the Beanstalk** story, for example:

Jack and the Beanstalk (Ladybird First Favourite Tales) Iona Treahy

Jack and the Baked Beanstalk Colin Stimpson

Jim and the Beanstalk Raymond Briggs

Jack and the Jelly Bean Stalk Rachael Mortimer (author) and Liz Pichon (illustrator)

Rhyme time

Encourage the class to learn this rhyme with you:

*Beanstalk, beanstalk, grows so high,
Grows and grows up to the sky.
Up climbs Jack, and doesn't stop,
Until he's climbed right to the top!*

UNIT 30: Reading comprehension lesson

3. Comprehension activities

Look at Student Book page 61 with the class. Tell the children to:

1. Complete the yes / no questions by circling the correct answer.

2. Read and answer the questions. Encourage the children to write in sentences.

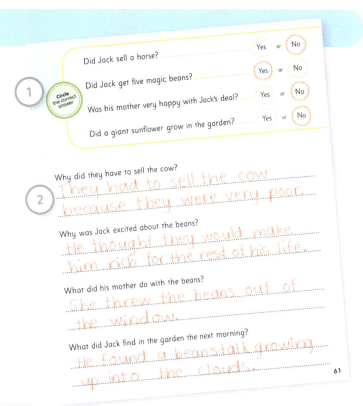

> **The children can also...**
> - Find all the words in the story with an <al> spelling, saying /or/.
> - Read the story with a partner.
> - Draw a picture and write a sentence from the story.

4. Plenary

Read the story again as a class. Encourage the children to use the punctuation to help them read with expression and fluency. Ask the children what they think Jack might find at the top of the beanstalk.

Further activities

- Grow some beans.
- Find out about, and taste, different sorts of beans.
- Make a picture using different sorts of dried beans.

Learning objectives

The children are learning to:
- Listen to, discuss, and recall details from story texts.
- Link what they hear or read to their own experiences.
- Become familiar with, and retell, traditional stories and rhymes.
- Discuss word meanings, linking new words to those they already know.
- Use inference and prediction.

UNIT 30: Writing skills lesson

Jack and the Beanstalk

 1. Introductory activity

Either read a version of the **Jack and the Beanstalk** story or re-read the story in the Student Book on page 60.

 2. Talk about the writing

Talk about the story **Jack and the Beanstalk**.

- How did Jack feel about selling the cow?
- Was Jack happy with the beans?
- Why did Jack think the beans were a good exchange for the cow?
- How did his mother feel when he got home and showed her the beans?
- How did Jack feel when his mother got cross and threw the beans out?
- What did Jack see when he looked out of the window the next morning and how did it make him feel?
- What did the beanstalk look like?

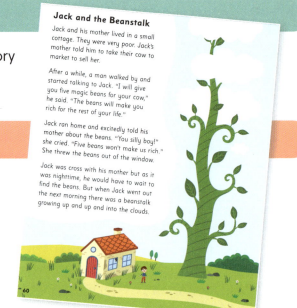

 3. Writing activity

Tell the children to plan and write their own version of **Jack and the Beanstalk**. They can retell the beginning of the story and then write about what they think happened when Jack got to the top of the beanstalk.

> **The children can also...**
> - Draw a set of pictures to illustrate their story.
> - Re-read their work, ensuring it makes sense.

 4. Plenary

Share some of the children's work, either by showing it to the other children or by asking some of them to read out what they have written.

134

UNIT 30: Writing skills lesson

 Further activities

- Measure different objects to find out what the tallest thing is in the classroom, or who the tallest person is in the class.
- Compare the size of some objects. (For example: *pencils, pieces of string, cuddly toys*.)
- Make paper beanstalks. Whose is the tallest?

 Assessment

 The child retells some of the story in sentences with some punctuation; uses correct or plausible spellings of most short and regular words.

 The child independently retells most of the story, writing in sentences and using details from the story they have read; uses correct spellings for known and regular words; uses plausible spellings for unknown and irregular words.

 The child independently retells most of the story, writing in sentences and using details from the story they have read, as well as adding their own ideas; uses correct spellings for known and regular words; makes plausible attempts at spelling unknown and irregular words.

Learning objectives

The children are learning to:
- Discuss what they are going to write about.
- Say a sentence.
- Write simple sentences to create a sequence of events (narrative).
- Write words using phonically plausible spellings.
- Re-read their writing to check that it makes sense.

135

UNIT 31: Reading comprehension lesson

Alice down the rabbit hole

 1. Read the story

Read the story to the class. Ensure the children can see the text, pointing to the words as you read. Read the story again, sounding out any difficult or unusual words, such as *disappear, peered,* and *strange.* Check that the children know the meaning of these words.

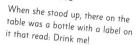

2. Talk about the story

> **Point out...**
>
> ...the phrase *Once upon a time* and explain that it is used at the beginning of many children's stories.

- What did Alice see?
- What happened to Alice?
- Where did she land?
- Why couldn't she open the doors?
- What could Alice see through the tiny door?
- What happened when Alice drank from the bottle? (*Remind the children that they should NOT drink from bottles that they do not know the contents of!*)

> **Explain that...**
>
> ...*drank* is the past tense of the verb *to drink,* and *shrank* is the past tense of *shrink.*

Story time

Further reading

Read other versions of stories and books about **Alice in Wonderland** and **Through the Looking-Glass** by Lewis Carroll. For example:

Alice's Adventures in Wonderland adapted by Saviour Pirotta and Amerigo Pinelli (illustrator)

Alice's Adventures in Wonderland adapted by Jeanne Willis and Ross Collins (illustrator)

Alice Through the Looking Glass adapted by Emma Chichester Clark

Rhyme time

Encourage the class to learn and repeat this rhyme with you:

> A rabbit raced a turtle,
> You know the turtle won,
> And Mr Bunny came in last,
> A little hot cross bun!

UNIT 31: Reading comprehension lesson

3. Comprehension activities

Look at Student Book page 63 with the class. Tell the children to:

1. Complete the yes / no questions by circling the correct answer.

2. Read and answer the questions. Encourage the children to answer by writing in sentences.

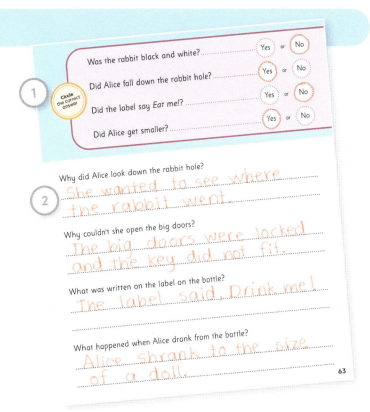

The children can also...
- Find all the words in the story with an <nk> spelling.
- Read the story with a partner.
- Draw a picture showing part of the story.

4. Plenary

Read the story again as a class. Encourage the children to use the punctuation to help them read with expression and fluency.

Further activities

- Draw a picture of a fantastic imaginary garden.
- Make miniature gardens in mason jars, teacups, or on saucers.
- Find out how to look after a plant.

Learning objectives

The children are learning to:
- Listen to, discuss, and recall details from stories.
- Link what they hear or read to their own experiences.
- Discuss word meanings, linking new words to those they already know.
- Use inference and prediction.

UNIT 31: Writing skills lesson

Alice down the rabbit hole

1. Introductory activity

Remind the children about the story of **Alice down the rabbit hole**. Point out that Alice started off big and tall, then became little and tiny after she drank what was in the bottle. Opposites like this are called *antonyms*.

2. Talk about the writing

The beginning of the story

- How might it feel to shrink down and become tiny?
- What did the hallway look like to Alice after she shrank?

The middle of the story

- What does Alice see when she goes through the tiny door into the garden?
- What are the flowers, trees, and animals like? Explain that because this is an imaginary (fictional) story the wildlife can be anything. (For example: *a chocolate tree, talking birds, magic multi-colored beans!*)
- Are the things in the garden tiny or is it just Alice? Is a blade of grass the size of a tree?
- Does Alice see the rabbit again?

The end of the story

- How could the story end?
- How might Alice get back home? (For example: *Alice goes back through the door and finds another bottle / Alice follows the rabbit down another rabbit hole and finds herself back in her own garden.*)

3. Writing activity

1. Tell the children they are going to write their own story about Alice falling down the rabbit hole. As the story is imaginary the children are going to start with the phrase *Once upon a time...* Write this on the board and ask how the sentence might end.
2. Choose one of the children's suggestions and model it on the board.
3. The children write their own version of the story. Encourage the children to write in sentences and remind them that their story needs to have a beginning, a middle, and an end.

The children can also...

- Draw pictures to illustrate their story.
- Re-read their work, ensuring it makes sense.

138

UNIT 31: Writing skills lesson

 4. Plenary

Share some of the children's work, either by showing it to the other children or by asking some of them to read out what they have written.

 Further activities

- Find out about, and read, more of Alice's adventures.
- Find more stories that start with, *Once upon a time...*
- Draw pictures to show what happens at the beginning, middle, and end of stories they know.

 Assessment

The child retells the story in their writing, using the characters of Alice and the rabbit, and attempts to continue the story; attempts to write in sentences with plausible spellings for most words, but little punctuation.

The child retells the story in their writing, using the characters of Alice and the rabbit, and continues the story as well as adding ideas of their own; thinks about the story having a beginning, middle, and end; writes at least a page independently using plausible spellings for most words and some periods.

The child retells the story in their writing, using the characters of Alice and the rabbit, and continues the story as well as adding ideas and characters of their own; thinks about the story having a beginning, middle, and end; writes at least two pages independently using correct spellings for most known and regular words; makes plausible attempts to spell unknown and irregular words.

Learning objectives

The children are learning to:
- Discuss what they are going to write about.
- Say a sentence.
- Write simple sentences to create a sequence of events (narrative).
- Write words using phonically plausible spellings.
- Re-read their writing to check that it makes sense.

Alice down the rabbit hole

139

UNIT 32: Reading comprehension lesson

Animal chatter

 1. Read the poem

Read the poem to the class. Ensure the children can see the text, pointing to the words as you read. Read the poem again, sounding out any difficult or unusual words, such as *Whee!, Boing!, prowl,* and *lair*. Check that the children know the meaning of these words. Point out all the speech marks and exclamation points.

Animal chatter

"Croak," said the frog, lost in the fog.
"Buzz," said the bee. "Look at me!"
"Quack," said the duck. "I'm in luck."
"Cheep," said the chick, pecking at the stick.
"I wish," said the raccoon, looking at the moon.
"Whee!" said the wombat, jumping off a hat.
"Woof," said the dog, stuck in a log.
"Boing," said the kangaroo. "I can spring too."
"Ouch!" said the snail, out in the hail.
"Wow!" said the earwig. "You are big."
"Mmmm," said the skunk, sitting in the junk.
"Whoosh!" said the whale, flapping its tail.
"Twit-twoo," said the brown owl, out on the prowl.
"Growl," said the bear, from inside its lair.
"Moo," said the cow, as she gave a bow.
"Blob," said the fish, and had a wish.

 2. Talk about the poem

- Ask the children if they can hear some of the rhyming words?
- Why are words like *Whee!* and *Wow!* followed by exclamation points?
- Why did the snail say *Ouch!*?
- What was the skunk doing?
- What did the raccoon say?
- Can the children say the word *growl* as if they are a bear?
- What, or who, might the earwig say is big?

Story time

Further reading

Read some silly stories, poems, or nonsense verse, for example:

I had a little Cat: Collected Poems for Children Charles Causley (author) and John Lawrence (illustrator)

Spring in the Yarm Fard Trevor Millum

Nonsense Verse of Lewis Carroll Lewis Carroll (author) and Lorna Hussey (illustrator)

Nonsense Verse of Edward Lear Edward Lear (author) and John Vernon Lord (illustrator)

Rhyme time

Encourage the class to learn this rhyme with you:

> *Bow-wow, goes the dog,*
> *Mew, mew, goes the cat,*
> *Croak, croak, goes the frog,*
> *And squeak goes the rat.*
>
> *Tu-whu, says the owl,*
> *Caw, caw, says the crow,*
> *Quack, quack, says the duck,*
> *And what cuckoos say—you know.*

UNIT 32: Reading comprehension lesson

3. Comprehension activities

Look at Student Book page 65 with the class. Tell the children to:

1. Complete the yes / no questions by circling the correct answer.
2. Read and answer the questions. Encourage the children to answer by writing in sentences.

> **The children can also...**
> - Read the poem with a partner, giving expression to what the animals say.
> - Draw a picture to illustrate one of the sentences.

4. Plenary

Read the poem again as a class. Encourage the children to read with expression and fluency. Different children could be chosen to read each line.

Further activities

- Draw illustrations of the animals in the poem.
- Think of sounds that the animals could make and how to write them.
- Write a nonsense version of the poem with the animals saying the "wrong" sounds. Look at **"Quack!" said the billy-goat** by Charles Causley for inspiration.

Learning objectives

The children are learning to:
- Listen to, discuss, and recall details from rhymes and poems.
- Link what they hear or read to their own experiences.
- Appreciate rhymes and poems, and recite some by heart.
- Discuss word meanings, linking new words to those they already know.

UNIT 32: Writing skills lesson

Animal chatter

> **Before class**
>
> If preferred or required, make sure the class has access to **Animal Chatter** (Jolly Phonics Reader, Yellow Level, General Fiction). If the class requires an e-book of this title, one can be downloaded from https://jollylearning.com/ereader-aep

1. Introductory activity

Talk about words that rhyme and sound similar to others. Discuss the idea that poems and rhymes can often be a bit silly and do not necessarily have to make sense, unlike most other types of writing. As a class, read **Animal Chatter**.

2. Talk about the writing

Think of some animals and some words that rhyme, or sound like, the animal's name. For example:

- Cat: hat, bat, sat
- Bird: herd, heard, word
- Fish / starfish: swish, squish, dish
- Crocodile: smile, mile, style
- Dinosaur: roar, four, store
- Raccoon: balloon, moon, spoon
- Fox: box, socks, locks

- Rabbit: habit, jacket, target
- Dolphin: bobbin, cabin, robin
- Ostrich: pitch, switch, twitch
- Elephant: elegant, excellent, accident
- Zebra: cheetah, meter, chatter
- Kangaroo: peekaboo, rescue, statue
- Flamingo: tornado, yellow, window

3. Writing activity

1. Tell the children to choose an animal and write its name down. This can be done individually or in pairs or small groups.
2. Then the children need to think of words that rhyme with, or sound similar to, the animal's name.
3. Next, the children think of something the animal might say and how to spell that sound or word.
4. They write the first line, like this, with the sound first, then the animal, then the word that rhymes with the animal:
   "Yowl!" said the fox, stuck in a box.

> **The children can also...**
> - Draw a set of pictures to illustrate other sets of sentences, then make a personal or class book of all of the pictures.
> - Design a cover for their personal or class book, including a title and their name as author.

142

UNIT 32: Writing skills lesson

 4. Plenary   **Further activities**

Share some of the children's work, either by showing it to the other children or by asking some of them to read out what they have written.

- Find out about different animals.
- Find the strangest animal or animal name that they can.
- Paint pictures of animals.
- Look at camouflage and the different patterns animals use to hide.

 Assessment

The child thinks of an animal and an appropriate sound for the animal to make; attempts to identify a rhyming word; attempts to make up a sentence with plausible spellings of most words and tries to use speech marks and punctuation.

The child thinks of appropriate animals and sounds they may make; identifies rhyming words; makes up sentences with rhyming words independently; uses speech marks and punctuation correctly; uses correct spellings for most regular and known words; makes plausible attempts at spelling irregular and unknown words.

The child thinks of an animal and an appropriate sound for the animal to make; identifies a rhyming word; makes up and writes a sentence with the rhyming word independently; uses most punctuation and speech marks correctly; uses correct spellings for most regular and known words; makes plausible attempts at spelling irregular and unknown words.

Learning objectives

The children are learning to:
- Discuss what they are going to write about.
- Understand the concept of rhyming words.
- Say a sentence.
- Write a simple sentence.
- Write words using phonically plausible spellings.
- Re-read their writing to check that it makes sense.

143

UNIT 33: Reading comprehension lesson

Bird spotting

 1. Read the story

Read the story to the class. Ensure the children can see the text, pointing to the words as you read. Read the story again, sounding out any difficult or unusual words, such as *whispered, murmured, replied, swirling, attraction,* and *bittern*. Check that the children know the meaning of these words. Briefly look at the punctuation and speech marks.

 2. Talk about the story

- What was Inky doing?
- Why did she tell Snake to be quiet?
- What is a spotter's list?
- What color clothes was the girl wearing?
- Why did the birds fly away?
- Did Snake enjoy birdwatching?
- What does Snake think is the best thing about birds?
- What words describe how someone was talking and can replace *said*?
- Have any of the class ever been birdwatching?

Story time

Further reading

Read some stories and books about birdwatching, for example:

National Trust: Out and About Bird Spotter
Robyn Swift (author) and Mike Langman (illustrator)

Bird Watching Journal for Kids
Clever Kid Press

The Children's Book of Birdwatching
Dan Rouse (author)

Rhyme time

Encourage the the class to learn this rhyme with you:

> Utter, answer, remark, exclaim.
> Chuckle, laugh, giggle, guffaw.
> Whisper, murmur, mumble, mutter.
> Scream, shout, yell, or holler.
> Said who?
> Said he, said she, said me!

UNIT 33: Reading comprehension lesson

3. Comprehension activities

Look at Student Book page 67 with the class. Tell the children to:

1. Complete the yes / no questions by circling the correct answer.
2. Read and answer the questions. Encourage the children to answer by writing in sentences, where appropriate.
3. Write down four words from the text that also mean *said*.

> **The children can also...**
> - Find all the words in the story with an <ir> spelling, saying /er/.
> - Read the story with a partner. *(Remind the children to read the words as they would be spoken, so murmured or whispered, for example.)*
> - Write a sentence from the story and draw a picture to illustrate the words.

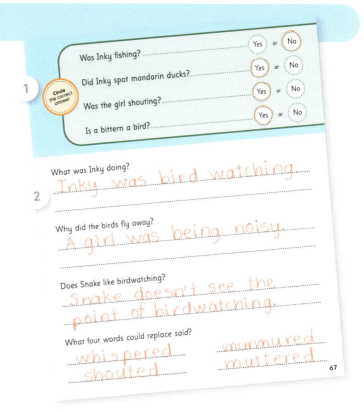

4. Plenary

Read the story again as a class. Encourage the children to read with expression and fluency.

Further activities

- Watch the birds out of the window and see if the children can identify some different species.
- Make a graph to show how many of each bird they spot.
- Find out about one of the birds they have seen.
- Make some bird feeders or bird food.

Learning objectives

The children are learning to:
- Listen to, discuss, and recall details from story texts.
- Link what they hear or read to their own experiences.
- Discuss word meanings, linking new words to those they already know.
- Use inference.
- Recite rhymes by heart.

145

Instead of *said*

1. Introductory activity

Discuss with the class the different words that can be used instead of *said*. Using different words makes writing more interesting and can better describe how a person was speaking. Ask the children to suggest words that describe **how** something was said. Write some of the suggested words on the board.

hinted
complained
joked

2. Talk about the writing

Choose one of the suggested words, for example *whisper*, and ask for a sentence that a person might whisper. Choose some other words and ask for sentences that might be said in those ways.

As well as adding extra detail, describing how something is said can add to the understanding of what is happening by the person reading the story.

On the board write the sentence:

"I am going out," said Inky.

Talk about where you are putting the speech marks and comma as you write the sentence. Read the sentence with the class. Then replace *said* with *whispered*. Read the sentence again with the children and tell them to make sure they whisper. Ask the children to suggest why Inky might whisper. (For example: *someone is asleep or concentrating on working or perhaps Inky does not want anyone to know what she is doing.*)

Then replace *whispered* with *yelled*. Discuss with the class the difference that change makes to the meaning of the sentence. Why might Inky be yelling? (For example: *she might be cross or the person she is telling is upstairs or has the television on loudly.*)

Try changing some other words and discuss the difference each change makes to the meaning of the sentence.

3. Writing activity

1. Tell the children to choose four words to use instead of *said*.
2. Then ask the children to think of a sentence for each word.
3. The children then write out the sentence using each word, or as many sentences as possible.

The children can also...

- Choose one of their sentences and use it as the start of a story. What happened next?

4. Plenary

Share some of the work by choosing a few children to read one of their sentences. Encourage them to say their sentence in the manner they described the words being said.

shouted

UNIT 33: Writing skills lesson

 Further activities

- Choose one sentence and draw a picture to illustrate it.
- Make a wall display of words that could be used instead of *said*. Each word could be written in a speech bubble in colored pen.
- Look at comics and books that involve speech. Make a display with some of them.

insisted

added

admitted

 Assessment

The child chooses four words and attempts to write a sentence using each word; writes some sentences with plausible spellings of most words and some punctuation.

The child chooses four words and writes a sentence using each word; each sentence reflects the meaning of the word used instead of *said*; chooses one of the sentences and begins to extend it into a story; sentences have correct punctuation and spellings of known and regular words; uses plausible spellings for unknown and irregular words.

The child chooses four words and writes a sentence using each word; each sentence reflects the meaning of the word used instead of *said*; chooses one of the sentences and begins to extend it into a story; sentences have mostly correct punctuation and spellings of known and regular words; uses plausible spellings for unknown and irregular words.

Learning objectives

The children are learning to:
- Discuss what they are going to write about.
- Say a sentence.
- Write simple sentences.
- Understand and use speech marks.
- Write words using phonically plausible spellings.
- Re-read their writing to check that it makes sense.

147

UNIT 34: Reading comprehension lesson

The enormous turnip

1. Read the fable

Read the fable to the class. Ensure the children can see the text, pointing to the words as you read. Read the story again, sounding out any difficult or unusual words, such as *vegetables* and *watching*. Check that the children know the meaning of these words.

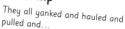

The enormous turnip

Arthur grew lots of vegetables in his garden. One of his turnips had grown enormous, so Arthur decided to pull up the turnip. He pulled and tugged and heaved, but the turnip did not move.

A nurse on her way home stopped to help Arthur. The two tried together, but the turnip did not move. A girl and her brother joined them, but their efforts were still no good.

Arthur's animals had been watching and they tried to help, too. His dog, with its purple collar, Arthur's turkey, his hen, and even his cat all got involved.

They all yanked and hauled and pulled and...

...suddenly the turnip shot out of the ground and all the people and animals tumbled into a heap!

To thank them all for their help and to help eat the turnip, Arthur invited everyone to dinner that evening.

68

2. Talk about the fable

- What did Arthur grow in his garden?
- Why did Arthur decide to pull up the turnip?
- Who tried to help Arthur?
- Why couldn't Arthur pull up the turnip by himself?
- What words mean the same as *pulled*?
- What happened when the turnip was finally pulled up?
- Why did Arthur invite everyone to dinner?
- Has anyone in the class ever eaten turnip?

Story time

Further reading

Read some stories and books about gardens, vegetables, and growing food, for example:

Eddie's Garden Sarah Garland

Where Does My Food Come From? Annabel Karmel (author) and Alex Willmore (illustrator)

Up in the Garden and Down in the Dirt Kate Messner (author) and Christopher Silas Neal (illustrator)

Rhyme time

Tell the children to make fists with both hands. As everyone recites the rhyme, one person uses a fist to gently touch all the other fists in turn. When a fist is touched on the word *out*, that child puts that fist behind their back. When both fists are behind their back, the child is out of the game. Keep going until only one fist or child is left. The children then say, "You're it!" and point to the remaining child, who then becomes the person to start the next game.

*One potato, two potato, three potato, four,
Five potato, six potato, seven potato, more.
O... U... T... spells OUT!*

UNIT 34: Reading comprehension lesson

3. Comprehension activities

Look at Student Book page 69 with the class. Tell the children to:

1. Complete the yes / no questions by circling the correct answer.
2. Read and answer the questions. Encourage the children to answer by writing in sentences, where appropriate.
3. Write down four words from the text that also mean *pulled*.

The children can also...
- Find all the words in the story with an <ur> spelling, saying /er/.
- Read the fable with a partner.
- Write a sentence from the story and draw a picture to illustrate the words.

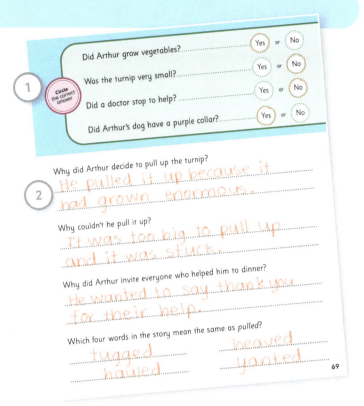

4. Plenary

Read the story again as a class. Encourage the children to read with expression and fluency.

Further activities

- Write a vegetable alphabet list poem.
- Taste turnips and other vegetables.
- Grow turnips.

Learning objectives

The children are learning to:
- Listen to, discuss, and recall details from story texts.
- Link what they hear or read to their own experiences.
- Become familiar with, and retell, traditional stories and rhymes.
- Discuss word meanings, linking new words to those they already know.

149

UNIT 34: Writing skills lesson

The enormous turnip

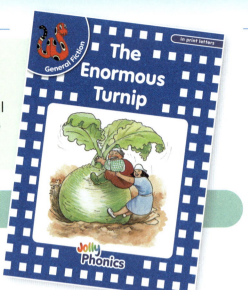

Before class
If preferred or required, make sure the class has access to **The Enormous Turnip** (Jolly Phonics Reader, Blue Level, General Fiction). If the class requires an e-book of this title, one can be downloaded from https://jollylearning.com/ereader-aep

1. Introductory activity

Remind the children of the story **The enormous turnip**. Or, as a class, read **The Enormous Turnip** (Jolly Phonics Reader, Blue Level, General Fiction) and point out that this is another version of the same story.

2. Talk about the writing

Talk about what happened at the beginning of the story when Arthur is introduced. He has a problem since he can't pull up the turnip by himself. In the middle of the story, various people and animals try to help Arthur pull up the turnip. At the end of the story, the turnip is pulled up and Arthur thanks everyone by inviting them to dinner.

Explain that...

...sometimes people write a new story based on another story but changing certain elements, including characters and important props. Instead of just retelling **The enormous turnip** their story could be about a different vegetable. Ask the children to suggest some different vegetables. (For example: *Inky could have grown an enormous carrot and had help pulling it up by Snake, Bee, a caterpillar, a robin, and some ants.*)

3. Writing activity

Tell the children to either retell the story of **The enormous turnip** or think up and write their own version of the story. Encourage the children to include lots of details, think about the words they use, to write in sentences, and to use correct punctuation.

The children can also...
- Draw a picture to illustrate the story.
- Re-read their work, ensuring it makes sense.

4. Plenary

Share some of the children's work, either by showing it to the other children or by asking some of them to read out what they have written.

UNIT 34: Writing skills lesson

 Further activities

- Find alternative versions of famous stories to read (or for the children to read themselves).
- Make a turnip print picture or use another vegetable, such as a potato.
- Find out about different vegetables and where they come from and how they are grown.
- Make a Mr Potato or Mr Turnip head or animal out of vegetables.

 Assessment

The child retells the story in order with most of the details correct; writes some sentences with plausible spellings of most words and some punctuation.

The child independently writes two or three pages in sentences of their own story based on the original; uses knowledge from that story, adding extra information and making changes to the original story and using punctuation; uses correct spellings for known and regular words and plausible spellings for unknown and irregular words.

The child retells the basic story with their writing or tells a similar story with only a few changes; writes one or two pages independently, with most punctuation correct and correct spellings of known and regular words; uses plausible spellings for unknown and irregular words.

Learning objectives

The children are learning to:
- Discuss what they are going to write about.
- Identify key features of a story to retell or adapt the text.
- Write simple sentences to create a sequence of events (narrative).
- Write words using correct or phonically plausible spellings.
- Re-read their writing to check that it makes sense.

UNIT 35: Reading comprehension lesson

Dinosaur names

1. Read the text

Read the text to the class. Ensure the children can see the words, pointing to them as you read. Read the passage again, sounding out any difficult or unusual words, such as *dinosaurs, scientist, monstrous, characteristic, pronunciation,* and *tyrant*. Check that the children know the meaning of these words. Explain that the forward slashes (/ /) around letters indicates that it is showing how the word is said, or pronounced.

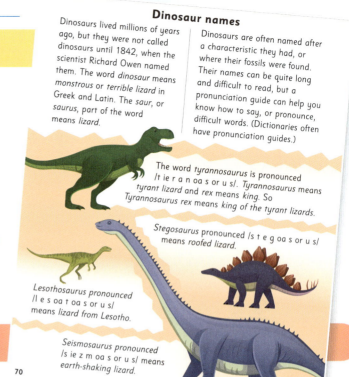

2. Talk about the text

- Are dinosaurs still alive today?
- What does the word *dinosaur* mean?
- How are dinosaurs named?
- What is a pronunciation guide?
- What does *Tyrannosaurus rex* mean?
- Why do you think *Seismosaurus* might be named that?
- If a dinosaur was found where the children lived, what might it be called?
- Do the children in the class know any dinosaur names?

Story time

Further reading

Read some stories and books about dinosaurs, for example:

The Dinosaur's Diary Julia Donaldson

Grannysaurus David Walliams (author) and Adam Stower (illustrator)

Hugasaurus James Allen and Amy Holman (authors) and Kah Yan Choong (illustrator)

My Encyclopedia of Very Important Dinosaurs Dorling Kindersley

My First Book of Dinosaurs Zoë Ingram (illustrator)

Joke time

Share these silly jokes with the class!

What do you call a dinosaur that is sleeping? A dino-snore!

What do you call a group of singing dinosaurs? A tyranno-chorus!

What kind of dinosaurs make good policemen? Tricera-cops!

UNIT 35: Reading comprehension lesson

3. Comprehension activities

Look at Student Book page 71 with the class. Tell the children to:

1. Complete the yes / no questions by circling the correct answer.
2. Read and answer the questions. Encourage the children to answer by writing in sentences.

> **The children can also...**
> - Find all the words in the text with an <au> spelling, saying /or/.
> - Read the passage with a partner.
> - Try and think up some interesting names for a dinosaur.

4. Plenary

Read the passage again as a class. Ask the children to read aloud the dinosaur names they have made up.

Further activities

- Find out about dinosaurs.
- Draw or paint pictures of dinosaurs.
- Look at the pronunciation guide for words in **Jolly Dictionary**.
- Find books with jokes and have a joke-telling session.

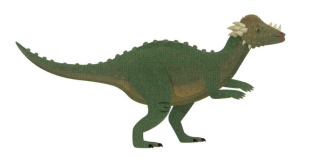

Learning objectives

The children are learning to:
- Listen to, discuss, and recall details from nonfiction.
- Discuss word meanings, linking new words to those they already know.
- Select different texts for a specific purpose.
- Use images to support their understanding of the text.
- Use inference.

Dinosaur names

153

UNIT 35: Writing skills lesson

Dinosaur names

1. Introductory activity

Talk about dinosaurs and dinosaur names with the class and look at some pictures of dinosaurs. Remind the children that the *saurus* part of the name is a Latin version of the Greek word *sauros*, which means *lizard*. (Latin is used for every animal's scientific name.) Tell the class that not all dinosaur names end with *saurus*, but many do.

2. Talk about the writing

Tell the class that they are going to make up a name for their own imaginary dinosaur. To make the dinosaur name, they are going to think of something, someone, or somewhere and add *saurus* on the end.

For example:

- *Sportyosaurus:* a dinosaur that likes sports
- *Splashosaurus:* a dinosaur that splashes in puddles and ponds
- *Stompasaurus:* a dinosaur that stomps everywhere
- *Hungryosaurus:* a dinosaur that is always hungry
- *Schoolasaurus:* a dinosaur that lives in schools

3. Writing activity

1. Tell the children to each choose a name for their dinosaur from those suggested, or to make up their own imaginary dinosaur name.
2. Give the children a short time to quickly draw a picture of their dinosaur.
3. Then, ask the children to write about what their dinosaur looks like, where it lives, and what it eats.

The children can also...

- Lay out some word cards, such as; *volcano, swamp, nest, eggs, help, rescue, stomp, forest, friendly, fierce, rocks, desert, weeds, lake*). The children choose a card and think of, and write, a sentence about their dinosaur using the word on the card.
- The children choose more cards and write more sentences.
- Re-read their work, ensuring it makes sense.

4. Plenary

Share some of the children's work, either by showing it to the other children or by asking some children to talk about their dinosaur.

154

UNIT 35: Writing skills lesson

Dinosaur names

 Further activities

- Look up what other dinosaur names mean.
- Make a prehistoric world in a shoebox with some model dinosaurs.
- Make dinosaur skeleton pictures from white paper straws.
- Make dinosaur footprint cookies.

 Assessment

The child chooses a dinosaur name from those suggested and writes some words and sentences about their dinosaur, such as where it lives and what it eats; uses correct spellings for most known words and short regular words; uses plausible spellings for irregular and unknown words.

The child makes up a dinosaur name on their own and writes sentences independently about their dinosaur, such as where it lives, what it eats and adds their own details; uses correct spellings for known words and regular words; uses plausible spellings for irregular and unknown words.

The child chooses a dinosaur name from those suggested or attempts to make one up and writes some sentences independently about their dinosaur, such as where it lives and what it eats; uses correct spellings for known words and regular words; uses plausible spellings for irregular and unknown words.

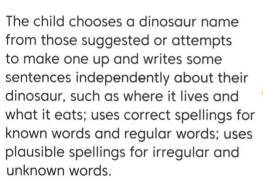

Learning objectives

The children are learning to:
- Discuss what they are going to write about.
- Understand different types of writing (nonfiction).
- Write simple sentences to create an informative text.
- Write words using phonically plausible spellings.
- Re-read their writing to check that it makes sense.

155

UNIT 36: Reading comprehension lesson

Strawberry sundae

 1. Read the recipe

Read the text to the class. Ensure the children can see the recipe, pointing to the words as you read. Read the text again, sounding out any difficult or unusual words, such as *sundae*, *sprig*, *optional*, *sauce*, *halves*, and *quarter*s. Check that the children know the meaning of these words. Point out the difference in spelling and capitalization of *sundae* and *Sunday*. These words sound the same, but have different spellings and different meanings. Proper nouns like *Sunday* start with a capital letter.

 2. Talk about the recipe

- What is an ice-cream sundae?
- What fruit does this ice-cream sundae have in it?
- What sort of ice cream is in the sundae?
- Why do you think the sundae has two different sorts of ice cream?
- Why does the recipe say to save two halves of a strawberry?
- How many pieces do you cut a strawberry into to make halves? And quarters?

- How is the sundae made?
- What does the recipe say to put on top of the sundae?
- What else could the children put on top?
- Why are there things on the top?

Story time

Further reading

Read some stories and books about ice cream, for example:

When Ice Cream Had a Meltdown
Michelle Robinson (author) and Tom Knight (illustrator)

Ketchup on My Sundae Nelleke Verhoeff

A Sundae with Everything on It
Kyle Scheele (author) and
Andy J. Pizza (illustrator)

Rhyme time

Encourage the class to learn this rhyme with you. The children can make up further verses.

" *I scream, you scream, we all scream for ice cream!*
Rah! Rah! Rah!
Tuesdays, Mondays, we all scream for sundaes,
Sis-boom-bah!
I scream, you scream, we all scream for ice cream!
Rah! Rah! Rah!
Strawberry, vanilla, we all scream for sundaes,
Sis-boom-bah!
I scream, you scream, we all scream for ice cream!
Rah! Rah! Rah!
Chocolate, caramel, we all scream for sundaes,
Sis-boom-bah!

156

UNIT 36: Reading comprehension lesson

 3. Comprehension activities

Look at Student Book page 73 with the class. Tell the children to:

1. Complete the yes / no questions by circling the correct answer.
2. Read and answer the questions. Encourage the children to answer by writing in sentences.

The children can also…
- Read the recipe with a partner.
- Talk about what they would like to add to the sundae.
- Draw a picture of their sundae in a tall sundae glass.

 4. Plenary

Read the recipe again as a class. Ask the children what other things they have thought of that could go in the sundae.

 Further activities

- Make ice-cream sundaes.
- Find out how ice cream is made.
- Look at and taste different fruits.

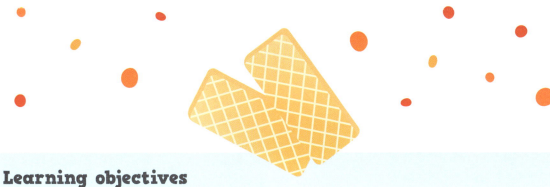

Learning objectives

The children are learning to:
- Listen to, discuss, and recall details from different types of text (recipe).
- Link what they hear or read to their own experiences.
- Discuss word meanings, linking new words to those they already know.
- Select different texts for a specific purpose.
- Use images to support their understanding of the text.
- Recite rhymes by heart.

157

Ice-cream sundaes

 ## 1. Introductory activity

Remind the class about the recipe for making a strawberry sundae. Ask the children what ingredients were needed and how the sundae was made.

 ## 2. Talk about the writing

- Has anyone had an ice-cream sundae and what flavor was it?
- What flavor ice cream did the sundae have in it?
- What flavor sauce did the sundae have in it?
- Did the sundae have fruit, sweets, or cookies?
- What did the sundae have on top? (For example: *wafers, sprinkles, nuts*.)
- Was the sundae in a tall glass and did they have a long spoon to reach the bottom of the glass?
- What are the children's favorite flavors?
- What do the children think would make a delicious ice-cream sundae flavor?
- What would their sundae have in it and what could they add?

 ## 3. Writing activity

1. Tell the children that they are going to think of their own ice-cream sundae recipe. They write the name of their sundae at the top of the page.
2. Then, ask the children to write the list of ingredients.
3. In steps in the right order, the children write how to make the sundae. Remind them to consider whether they need to cut up anything, which things to add in what order, and what they are going to put on the top of their sundae.

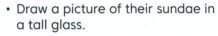

The children can also...

- Draw a picture of their sundae in a tall glass.
- Label the sundae's layers and the visible ingredients.
- Show how the sundae's top is decorated.
- Re-read their work, ensuring it makes sense.

 ## 4. Plenary

Share some of the children's work, either by showing it to the other children or by asking some of them to talk about their ice-cream sundae.

UNIT 36: Writing skills lesson

  Further activities

- Make a graph of favorite ice-cream flavors.
- Find recipes for other types of sundaes, such as banana splits and knickerbocker glories.
- Think of, and draw, a yucky sundae with disgusting flavors and decorations.

 Assessment

The child thinks of a possible flavor for an ice-cream sundae and writes words and sentences, including a list of ingredients and some labels or annotations; uses correct spellings for known words and short regular words; uses plausible spellings for unknown and irregular words as well as longer regular words.

The child thinks of a possible flavor for an ice-cream sundae and writes sentences independently, including a list of ingredients, how to make the sundae, some labels or annotations, and adds some of their own details; uses correct spellings for known and regular words; uses plausible spellings for unknown and irregular words.

The child thinks of a possible flavor for an ice-cream sundae and writes sentences independently, including a list of ingredients, some labels or annotations, and adds some of their own details; uses correct spellings for known and regular words; uses plausible spellings for unknown and irregular words.

Learning objectives

The children are learning to:
- Discuss what they are going to write about.
- Use a simple plan (a recipe) to support or organize writing.
- Write an informative text with labels and annotations.
- Write words using phonically plausible spelling.
- Re-read their writing, ensuring it makes sense.